EASONS
Winter Recipes

A selection of Seasonal Recipes including Vegetarian which are all Calorie Counted and based on the Weight Watchers Programme

First Published 1991 by Weight Watchers (U.K.) Ltd.

For information about Weight Watchers classes, contact:

Weight Watchers (U.K.) Ltd.,
Kidwells Park House
Kidwells Park Drive
Maidenhead, Berkshire SL6 8YT

Telephone: Maidenhead (0628) 777077

Photography by Simon Smith
Edited, and preparation of food for photography by Ann Page-Wood
Graphic Design by Tony Durrant
Production by The Marine Press Ltd., Surbiton, Surrey
Illustrations by Christine Howell

Photosetting and repro by Michael Weintroub Graphics Ltd, Kenton, Middlesex.
Printed and bound by Philip Print Ltd, London NW10.

$\mathscr{C}$ONTENTS

About our Recipes

Weight Watchers members enjoy a wide variety of recipes while following the Weight Watchers Programme. The 'Seasons' Collection consists of recipes chosen to include ingredients which are in plentiful supply and at their cheapest at certain times of the year. 'Winter' is the third of the series, and the recipes have been compiled especially for you, but are suitable for non-members who enjoy good food and simple, practical recipes.

★ Selections are shown so you can fit the recipes into your Weight Watchers Food Plan and we've calorie counted them too.

★ Accuracy in weighing ingredients ensures successful results and leads to good weight control.

★ Use either the imperial or metric measurements – don't mix the two.
1 teaspoon   = 5ml
1 tablespoon = 15ml

★ Make sure ingredients measured with a spoon are levelled by using the back of a knife.

★ Drain canned fish thoroughly.

★ Buy the leanest cuts of meat and, when possible, remove the skin from poultry before cooking.

★ Canned fruit should be in natural juice with no sugar added.

☆ This symbol indicates recipes which may be used by Vegetarian as well as Non-Vegetarian members.

Happy cooking!

Introduction

This book comprises recipes which are particularly well suited for cooking throughout the winter months. For the purpose of this book we have decided to call December, January and February the "Winter months" although, with our unpredictable climate, it frequently starts earlier and seems to drag on longer!

Christmas is probably the most widely celebrated festival and we have included recipes for the Christmas Meal, including a delicious pudding. Other festivals, such as Easter, have not been given great emphasis but many recipes are suitable for serving at that time. Pancakes, for example, are the traditional fare for Shrove Tuesday, Pancake Day, and there is a recipe for Pancakes which can be served on their own or with lemon juice and sugar as well as the more spectacular Crêpes Suzette.

Compared with the Summer and Spring months there is not such a wide variety of home-grown fruit and vegetables. However many fruits, for example the citrus fruits and vegetables, are imported to give additional choice. It is during these months that frozen and canned produce are particularly useful but remember to always check additional sugar has not been added during processing.

The following notes give some details of fruit and vegetables which will be on sale during the Winter.

FRUIT

Apples

Apples, which have been picked in the Autumn, may be wrapped and kept in a cool place with a good circulation of air for many weeks so the home-grown favourites can be enjoyed throughout the Winter months. Cooking apples, such as the Bramley's Seedling, may be baked or stewed. Dessert apples, such as the well-known Cox's Orange Pippin, may be eaten raw or cooked.

CITRUS FRUITS

The wide range of citrus fruit seems to grow larger every year. Some years ago oranges, lemons, grapefruits and tangerines would have been considered 'the citrus fruits' but now many others are imported and the choice has increased as many hybrids have been introduced. The following list includes a few of the best known varieties.

Clementines, Tangerines, Satsumas and Mandarins

These fruits have loose skins and are therefore easily peeled. They are eaten raw and may be included in sweet or savoury salads.

Grapefruit, Pomelo and Ugli

These fruits are usually eaten uncooked. The Pomelo, also known as Shaddock, is the largest of the citrus fruits and has a particularly thick skin. The Ugli is a hybrid between the grapefruit and tangerine. It is a rough-skinned unattractive fruit which has a sweeter flavour than the grapefruit.

Kumquats

These are the smallest citrus fruits. They are small and oval with a bright orange smooth skin. They may be eaten raw in salads but are occasionally served in cooked dishes. The whole fruit; zest, juice and pips, is edible. The fruit has a sweet-sour flavour.

Lemons and Limes

Everyone must be familiar with lemons and, although they are available throughout the year, they are traditionally served with pancakes on Shrove Tuesday. Lime juice and zest may be used in place of lemon in some recipes.

Oranges

Sweet oranges are available all the year but Blood Oranges, which have a slightly rough skin and a bright flesh speckled with red, and the bitter Seville Orange, are associated with Winter. The Seville Orange is available in January and February and is primarily used in marmalade.

Custard Apples

These fruits are becoming more widely available and are at their best from the Autumn through to Spring. Cut the fruit in half and scoop out the flesh, the seeds are not edible.

Dates

Fresh dates are available from September to March. They may be served raw or cooked. To serve whole, the stalk should be pinched off then, by gently squeezing the opposite end, the stone can be removed.

Lychees

A few years ago lychees were unknown to the majority of people but now they are sold widely during December, January and February. They have a rough pinky coloured brittle skin which has to be peeled off. They may be served raw or cooked.

Persimmons

These fruits are available from late Autumn until mid-Winter. To obtain the best flavour the fruit must be really ripe and fleshy.

Rhubarb

Forced rhubarb is available during the Winter months. This rhubarb is a pretty pink colour. Although strictly a vegetable rhubarb is served as a fruit. It is always eaten cooked and care should be taken not to overcook or the stems will collapse.

VEGETABLES

Brussels Sprouts

Brussels sprouts have been described as miniature cabbages. They grow from woody stalks and should be harvested while still firm tight buds. To prepare the sprouts, trim the base and remove any loose outer leaves then cut a cross in the base. Boil or steam until cooked. The leaves at the top of the stalk, Brussels Tops, are served in the same way as cabbage.

Chinese Leaves, Kale and Cabbages

Chinese Leaves or Chinese Cabbage are sold from December to March. They may be eaten in the same way as lettuce, raw or cooked. Kale is dark green with a frilly edge to the leaves. It is usually cooked. There are many varieties of cabbages available throughout the Winter. They may be eaten raw in salads, steamed, boiled or baked.

Kholrabi

The kholrabi belongs to the cabbage family. It is not a root vegetable, it is the swollen base of a stem. There are many varieties of the kholrabi, some green, others purple. Their texture is similar to a delicate turnip. The bulb as well as the young leaves may be eaten steamed, boiled, or raw in salads.

Lamb's Lettuce

Lamb's Lettuce is also known as Mache and Corn Salad. The small green leaves are available from November to March. They should be washed then shaken dry and eaten raw in a salad or used to decorate dishes.

ROOT VEGETABLES

Carrots

Although carrots are available throughout the year they are particularly useful during the Winter as their bright colour makes an attractive addition to hot and cold meals.

Celeriac

Choose smooth skinned celeriac, add a little lemon juice during cooking to help maintain its creamy white colour.

Jerusalem Artichokes

This tuberous knobbly vegetable may be eaten raw or cooked. It is available from Winter to early Summer. As its creamy white flesh discolours during preparation and cooking, add a little lemon juice to the cooking water. Uncooked Jerusalem Artichokes, which are to be eaten in salads, may be tossed in a lemon juice dressing to help prevent browning.

Parnips

Parsnips can be served in a wide variety of ways; small parsnips may be boiled, steamed or roasted but the older variety which tends to have a slightly 'woody' central core, are ideal for pureés and soups.

Potatoes

The maincrop potatoes store well and are available throughout the Winter. There are many varieties, but for cooking purposes they are best suited to boiling as they have a floury texture, but the reds are ideal for baking. They may be served as jacket potatoes baked in their skins and served as a vegetable accompaniment to a main course, or filled to make the main meal component of a snack or main meal. Potatoes may be steamed, boiled and mashed or cooked and incorporated in a variety of salads. Chips or deep-fried potatoes are not suitable for anyone wishing to lose weight, as they absorb fat and are high in calories.

Swede

Swedes are members of the cabbage family. The most common variety has a yellow flesh with a mauvey-yellow skin. Swedes should be firm, feel heavy for their size and have smooth skins. They may be eaten steamed, boiled or roasted. They make unusual accompaniments to main meals when puréed and served on their own or mixed with other vegetables.

FRUIT

Buttermilk Refresher ☆

Serves 2
65 Calories per serving

Ingredients:

½ medium banana
2oz (60g) drained canned apricots
¼ pint (150ml) buttermilk
2-3 drops vanilla essence
1 teaspoon clear honey
ground cinnamon

Method:

1) Place the banana and apricots in the goblet of a liquidiser.

2) Add the buttermilk, vanilla essence and honey to the fruits then process until smooth and frothy.

3) Pour the Buttermilk Refresher into two glasses and sprinkle cinnamon over. Serve immediately.

Selections per serving: ¾ Fruit, ¼ Milk, 10 Optional Calories

TIP: *Serve the remaining banana at breakfast, chopped in small pieces and mixed with cereal.*

Chocolate Pear Condé ☆

Serves 4
175 Calories per serving

Ingredients:

For the rice:
2oz (60g) pudding rice
1 pint (600ml) skimmed milk
1 tablespoon sugar

For the chocolate sauce:
approximately ¼ pint (150ml) skimmed milk
2 teaspoons cornflour
1 tablespoon cocoa
1 tablespoon sugar

4 medium fresh or drained canned pears
2 teaspoons desiccated coconut

Method:

1) Make the rice pudding according to the recipe on page 47, do not double the quantities as the recipe will serve four when it is incorporated with the other ingredients. Leave the rice pudding until cold.

2) Make the chocolate sauce. Pour ¼ pint (150ml) skimmed milk into a measuring jug. Blend the cornflour, cocoa and sugar to a paste with a little of the measured milk. Pour the remaining milk into a small saucepan and heat until steaming then pour onto the cocoa mixture, stirring all the time.

3) Pour the chocolate sauce back into the saucepan and bring to the boil, stirring all the time, boil for 1-2 minutes.

4) Pour the chocolate sauce into a bowl or jug and cover with a damp piece of greaseproof paper, leave until cold.

5) Spoon a quarter of the cold rice into four serving glasses. If using fresh pears peel, quarter then remove the cores. Place one pear on top of each portion of rice.

6) Remove the greaseproof paper from the cold chocolate sauce and whisk with a fork until smooth – if the sauce is very thick whisk in one tablespoon skimmed milk.

7) Spoon the chocolate sauce over the pears, sprinkle over the coconut and serve.

Selections per serving: ½ Bread, 1 Fruit, ½ Milk, 60 Optional Calories

Creamy Fruit Dessert☆

Ingredients:

½ pint (300ml) skimmed milk
1½oz (45g) flaked rice
aritificial sweetener
3 tablespoons double cream
4oz (120g) fresh or drained canned pineapple
4oz (120g) drained canned mandarins

Method:

1) Heat the milk in a small saucepan until steaming, sprinkle in the flaked rice and bring to the boil, stirring all the time.

2) Turn the heat as low as possible and continue cooking and stirring for about 10 minutes until the mixture is thick. Remove from the heat and sweeten to taste with artificial sweetener. Set aside until cold.

3) Stir the cream into the cold thick rice then gradually mix in the fruit. If the mixture remains very thick add a little of the canned fruit juice. Spoon into four serving glasses and chill until required.

Selections per serving: ¼ Bread, ½ Fruit, ¼ Milk, 50 Optional Calories

TIP: *If your Optional Calories allow, sprinkle a little grated white chocolate over the Chocolate Topped Bananas.*

Chocolate-Topped Bananas☆

Ingredients:

2 tablespoons cocoa
1oz (30g) cornflour
½ pint (300ml) skimmed milk
artificial sweetener
4 tablespoons rum
4 medium bananas

Method:

1) Blend the cocoa and cornflour to a paste with 3-4 tablespoons milk.

2) Heat the remaining milk in a small saucepan until steaming, stir a little of the hot milk into the cornflour mixture then pour into the saucepan and bring to the boil, stirring all the time. Boil for 1-2 minutes.

3) Pour the chocolate sauce into a jug or bowl and sweeten to taste with artificial sweetener. Cover the sauce with a piece of damp greaseproof paper. Leave until cold.

4) Remove the paper from the sauce and whisk in the rum, a tablespoon at a time.

5) Thinly slice the bananas and divide between four serving glasses. Spoon the thick rum and chocolate mixture over and serve.

Selections per serving: ¼ Bread, 2 Fruit, ¼ Milk, 50 Optional Calories

Exotic Fruit Salad ☆

Ingredients:

3oz (90g) dried stoned prunes
2½oz (75g) dried fruit e.g. apple rings, apricots
2 medium oranges
1 medium carambola (star fruit)
1 medium persimmon
4 lychees
4oz (120g) fresh pineapple
4 medium kumquats
3 fresh dates
1½oz (45g) seedless grapes
½ medium grapefruit

Method:

1) Place the dried fruit in a bowl. Squeeze the juice from the oranges and pour over the fruit, add sufficient cold water to completely cover the fruit. Leave the fruit to stand at least 8 hours. If possible add more water to cover the fruit and leave longer so it becomes very plump.

2) Place the soaked dried fruit into a small saucepan, add additional water to cover the fruit then cover the saucepan and simmer over a low heat for about 10 minutes, leave to cool.

3) Thinly slice the carambola.

4) Cut the persimmon into wedges and peel then stone the lychees.

5) Cut the pineapple into ¾ inch (2cm) cubes and halve the kumquats.

6) Slide the skin off the dates, halve, then remove the stones.

7) Leave very small grapes whole, cut larger ones in half. Cut the peel off the grapefruit and divide into segments removing as much membrane as possible.

8) Mix all the fruit together in a bowl, pour over the liquid remaining in the saucepan and chill until ready to serve.

Selections per serving: 2¼ Fruit, 10 Optional Calories

TIP: *If carambolas are unavailable, substitute half a medium papaya or mango.*

Stuffed Dates ☆

Ingredients:

2 tablespoons crunchy peanut butter
2oz (60g) curd cheese
1 tablespoon buttermilk
grated zest of ¼-½ medium orange
8 fresh dates

Method:

1) Mix together the peanut butter, curd cheese and buttermilk. Add grated orange zest to taste.

2) Split the dates lengthways, remove the stone keeping each date whole.

3) Spoon or pipe the peanut butter filling into each date.

Selections per serving: ½ Fat, 1 Fruit, ¾ Protein,
                          5 Optional Calories

Exotic Fruit Salad

Christmas Pudding

Christmas Pudding ☆

Ingredients:

1 teaspoon margarine
6oz (180g) fresh breadcrumbs
2oz (60g) flour
12oz (360g) dried fruit
grated zest of 1 lemon
½ teaspoon allspice
½ teaspoon cinnamon
1½oz (45g) carrot, finely grated
1oz (30g) soft brown sugar
1 tablespoon treacle
1½ teaspoons brandy flavouring
2 large eggs

Method:

1) Grease a 1½ pint (900ml) basin with the margarine.

2) Mix the breadcrumbs together with the flour, dried fruit, lemon zest, spices, carrot and sugar.

3) Spoon the treacle into a jug, add the brandy flavouring and eggs then whisk until evenly combined.

4) Mix the egg mixture into the dried ingredients.

5) Spoon the mixture into the prepared basin, press down with the back of a spoon then cover with a layer of pleated non-stick baking parchment and foil. Steam for 1 hour 45 minutes.

6) Carefully lift the basin from the saucepan or steamer and remove the paper and foil. Invert the pudding onto a serving plate and decorate with a sprig of holly.

N.B. This pudding does not have the keeping quality of the traditional pudding which is very rich and contains a high proportion of fat, therefore make it on Christmas Day or Christmas Eve and then reheat it on Christmas Day.

Selections per serving: 1 Bread, 1½ Fruit, ¼ Protein, 25 Optional Calories

---

TIP: *Serve the Sunshine Salad with a mixture of cream and yogurt, but remember to add the additional Optional Calories*

Sunshine Salad ☆

Ingredients:

8oz (240g) fresh pineapple
6oz (180g) kumquats
12 lychees

Method:

1) Cut the pineapple into ¾ inch (2cm) chunks.

2) Cut the kumquats in half.

3) Peel the lychees then cut in half and remove the stones.

4) Mix all the prepared fruits together and divide between four serving glasses or dishes.

Selections per serving: 1½ Fruit

Rhubarb and Custard ☆

Ingredients:

12oz (360g) rhubarb
3 tablespoons low-calorie orange juice
artificial sweetener

For the custard:
1 tablespoon custard powder
½ pint (300ml) skimmed milk
2 teaspoons sugar

Method:

1) Cut the rhubarb into 1-1½ inch (2.5-4cm) lengths.

2) Place the rhubarb and orange juice in a small saucepan and cook over a very low heat until the rhubarb is cooked but still in pieces. Sweeten to taste with artificial sweetener.

3) While the rhubarb is cooking make the custard. Blend the custard powder to a smooth paste with a little milk.

4) Heat the remaining milk in a small saucepan until steaming then pour onto the blended mixture. Return the milk and custard powder to the saucepan and bring to the boil stirring all the time. Boil for 2 minutes. Stir in the sugar.

5) Place the rhubarb in serving bowls and serve the custard separately.

Selections per serving: ½ Milk, 40 Optional Calories

TIP: *If preferred, the fruit used in the Boil-Bake Cake may be simmered in weak black tea.*

Boil-Bake Cake ☆

Ingredients:

14fl oz (420ml) water
10½oz (315g) mixed dried fruit
6oz (180g) caster sugar
7 tablespoons margarine
1 teaspoon mixed spice
14oz (420g) self-raising flour
1 teaspoon bicarbonate of soda
pinch of salt

Method:

1) Line a 7 inch (17.5cm) deep cake tin with non-stick baking parchment, leaving at least 1 inch (2.5cm) of paper above the level of the tin.

2) Heat the water, mixed fruit, sugar, margarine and mixed spice gently, simmer for 10 minutes, stirring occasionally. Leave to cool.

3) Sieve the flour, bicarbonate of soda and salt into a bowl. Beat in the cool fruit mixture . Transfer to the prepared tin and bake immediately in a preheated oven, 350F, 180C, Gas Mark 4 for 1 hour 30 minutes – 1 hour 40 minutes. Leave to cool for 5 minutes then transfer to a cooling rack until cold. Cut into 14 slices.

Selections per serving: 1 Bread, 1½ Fat, ¾ Fruit,
                          50 Optional Calories

Mulled Wine ☆

Ingredients:

1 x 750ml bottle red wine
3 medium oranges
4fl oz (120ml) water
3 inch (7.5cm) stick of cinnamon
4 cloves
3oz (90g) sugar

Method:

1) Pour the wine into a saucepan.

2) Squeeze the juice from two oranges.

3) Stir the orange juice into the wine, add the water and sugar.

4) Crumble the cinnamon into the saucepan and add the cloves.

5) Gently heat the wine mixture and leave to simmer gently for 12-15 minutes.

6) Strain the steaming Mulled Wine into eight glasses or a punch bowl, thinly slice the remaining orange and add to the glasses or bowl.

Selections per serving: ¼ Fruit, 125 Optional Calories

TIP: *Serve the Mulled Wine at special occasions throughout the year. It makes an ideal drink for Hallowe'en night.*

Saucy Mango ☆

Ingredients:

1 firm medium mango
1½ tablespoons margarine
1oz (30g) flour
½ pint (300ml) skimmed milk
1 tablespoon concentrated frozen orange juice
lemon juice

Method:

1) Cut the mango lengthways, about ½ inch (1.25cm) off centre. Peel away the skin then cut the fruit into ½ inch (1.25cm) cubes. Cut the other side of the mango and cut into cubes. Peel the skin from the centre slice of mango, then cut the fruit into cubes.

2) Melt the margarine in a saucepan, add the flour and stir round then remove from the heat.

3) Gradually blend in the milk, add the concentrated orange juice and bring to the boil stirring all the time. Add the mango and return to the boil. Simmer over a low heat, stirring frequently, for 10-15 minutes depending on the firmness of the mango.

4) Remove the Saucy Mango from the heat, add the lemon juice to taste then spoon into four small ramekins.

Selections per serving: ¼ Bread, 1 Fat, ½ Fruit, ¼ Milk, 15 Optional Calories

Kumquat Refresher ☆

Ingredients:

1 tablespoon sugar
6 tablespoons water
thin strip of lemon zest
1 teaspoon orange flower water
sprig of mint
8 medium kumquats, halved through the centre,
    not lengthways
4oz (120g) fresh pineapple cubes

Method:

1) Place the sugar, water and lemon zest in a small saucepan. Heat gently until the sugar has dissolved, then boil fiercely for 1 minute.

2) Remove from the heat and stir in the orange flower water, mint, kumquats and pineapple. Leave to cool.

3) Remove the lemon zest before serving.

Selections per serving: 1 Fruit, 30 Optional Calories

TIP: *Use the remaining half banana in the Buttermilk Refresher (Page 10).*

Tropical Salad ☆

Ingredients:

For the salad:
1 lime
4 teaspoons sugar
1 teaspoon orange flower water
6 tablespoons water
½ medium papaya
½ medium banana
3 lychees
1½oz (45g) black grapes, halved and seeded
4 dates, stoned and halved
1 kiwi fruit, sliced

For the sauce:
4 tablespoons soured cream
4 tablespoons low-fat natural yogurt
1 teaspoon clear honey

Method:

1) Remove the zest from the lime with a zester, wrap a few strips in clingfilm and reserve. Place the remainder in a saucepan with the sugar, orange flower water and water. Heat gently until the water boils, allow to boil for 1-2 minutes, then leave to cool.

2) Squeeze the juice from the lime.

3) Scoop out and discard the black seeds from the papaya, then cut off the skin. Cut the flesh into chunks.

4) Peel and slice the banana and toss in the lime juice.

5) Peel the skin from the lychees, cut them in half and remove the stones.

6) Mix together the papaya, banana, lychees, grapes, dates and kiwi fruit, pour over the cool syrup and divide between four serving dishes.

7) Mix the sauce ingredients together, transfer to a small bowl and scatter the reserved lime zest over the top.

Selections per serving: 1½ Fruit, 85 Optional Calories

Apricot Sundae ☆

Ingredients:

8oz (240g) drained canned apricots plus
2 tablespoons juice
2 teaspoons cornflour
artificial sweetener
5fl oz (150ml) very low-fat vanilla yogurt

Method:

1) Place the apricots in the goblet of a liquidiser and process to a purée.

2) Gradually blend the apricot juice together with the cornflour, stir in the apricot purée.

3) Pour the apricot mixture into a small saucepan and bring to the boil, stirring all the time. Boil for 1-2 minutes then remove from the heat and allow to cool.

4) Sweeten the apricot mixture with artificial sweetener.

5) Whisk or stir the vanilla yogurt into the cool apricot mixture. Spoon into two serving dishes. Serve chilled.

Selections per serving: 1 Fruit, 60 Optional Calories

TIP: *Serve either of these desserts with a scoop of real dairy ice-cream – but remember to add the Optional Calories.*

Hot Apple Rings ☆

Ingredients:

2 medium cooking apples
2 medium satsumas
lemon juice
1 teaspoon margarine
2 teaspoons sugar

Method:

1) Core then peel the apples, place in a saucepan.

2) Halve then squeeze the juice from the satsumas and add to the apple. Add a ¼ teaspoon lemon juice.

3) Cover the saucepan and place over a low heat. Gently simmer the apple rings for about 4 minutes until cooked but firm.

4) Transfer the rings and the cooking juices to a flameproof dish. Dot the margarine over the rings and sprinkle with the sugar.

5) Place the dish under a preheated very hot grill and cook until beginning to turn golden brown. Serve immediately.

Selections per serving: ½ Fat, 1½ Fruit, 20 Optional Calories

Raspberry Jelly Sundae ☆

Serves 6
125 Calories per serving

Ingredients:

1 tablet raspberry jelly
15¼oz (432g) can crushed pineapple
4oz (120g) fromage frais
4oz (120g) banana

Method:

1) Break the jelly into small pieces then place in a measuring jug. Pour boiling water into the jug to the 4fl oz (120ml) mark. Stir round until the jelly has completely dissolved.

2) Stir all of the crushed pineapple into the dissolved jelly then chill for several hours until set.

3) Whisk the jelly to break the set, add the fromage frais and whisk once again.

4) Chop the banana and stir into the jelly mixture then spoon into six serving glasses. Chill until completely set.

Selections per serving: 1 Fruit, ¼ Protein, 70 Optional Calories

TIP: *Try using wholemeal flour and demerara sugar to make an interesting crumble topping.*

Rhubarb and Apple Crumble ☆

Serves 4
235 Calories per serving

Ingredients:

2 medium apples
½ teaspoon ground ginger
12-14oz (360-420g) rhubarb (cut in 1½ inch (4cm) lengths
3 tablespoons water
artificial sweetener
4oz (120g) flour
3 tablespoons margarine
1 tablespoon sugar

Method:

1) Peel, quarter then core the apples then cut each quarter in half.

2) Place the apples in the base of a saucepan, sprinkle over the ginger then add the rhubarb and lastly the water. Cover the saucepan and cook over a very low heat for about 8 minutes until the fruit is a little firm but almost cooked. Spoon the fruit into a deep ovenproof dish and sweeten to taste with artificial sweetener.

3) Sieve the flour into a bowl and add the margarine, if possible margarine which has been stored in the freezer, then rub in until the mixture resembles fresh breadcrumbs. Stir in the sugar.

4) Sprinkle the crumble topping over the fruit then transfer to the oven and bake at 375F, 190C, Gas Mark 5 for 15-20 minutes.

Selections per serving: 1 Bread, 2 Fat, ½ Fruit, 25 Optional Calories

Prune Mousse ☆

Ingredients:

10oz (300g) prunes
½ pint (300ml) weak tea
6oz (180g) fromage frais (8% fat)
2 teaspoons caster sugar
5 tablespoons sweet sherry
½ tablespoon gelatine
1 large egg white
pinch of cream of tartar

Method:

1) Place the prunes in a bowl, cover with the tea and leave to soak for 6 hours.

2) Transfer the prunes to a saucepan and bring to the boil, cover and leave over a low heat for 15-20 minutes or until cooked – if necessary add a little additional water. Leave until cool.

3) Remove all the stones from the prunes then transfer to the goblet of a liquidiser, add the fromage frais, sugar and sherry and process to a purée, there should just be just over a pint (600ml) of thick purée.

4) Spoon 2 tablespoons hot water into a cup or small basin, sprinkle the gelatine into the water and stir well then stand in a saucepan and leave until completely dissolved.

5) Stir the dissolved gelatine into the prune purée and leave until beginning to set.

6) Whisk the egg white together with the cream of tartar until peaking then gently fold into the purée. Spoon into serving glasses and chill until completely set.

Selections per serving: 1½ Fruit, ½ Protein, 30 Optional Calories

⊘⊘

TIP: *Use vegetable based setting agent for the Prune Mousse when serving vegetarians.*

⊘⊘

Banana Brandy Yogurt ☆

Ingredients:

2 medium bananas
5fl oz (150ml) low-fat hazelnut yogurt
1 tablespoon brandy
pinch of ground allspice

Method:

1) Cut one of the bananas in half. Mash one whole banana and one of the halves until smooth.

2) Gradually mix in the hazelnut yogurt then stir in the brandy and allspice.

3) Cut the remaining banana half into small dice and stir into the brandy and yogurt mixture.

4) Just before serving stir the banana mixture then spoon into two serving glasses.

Selections per serving: 2 Fruit, 65 Optional Calories

Pear Snowballs ☆

Ingredients:

3 tablespoons double cream
2oz (60g) fromage frais (8% fat)
½ tablespoon strawberry conserve, sieved
2 medium ripe pears
1 teaspoon desiccated coconut

Method:

1) Spoon the cream into a small bowl and whisk until thick and it holds its own shape.

2) In a separate bowl mix the fromage frais together with the strawberry conserve.

3) Peel the pears and, using a sharp knife, remove the core by cutting with the blade at an angle so it removes a cone shape from each pear. Leave the stalk in position and stand the pears upright on two serving plates. If necessary remove a very thin slice from each pear so it stands firmly upright.

4) Carefully stir the fromage frais mixture into the thick cream.

5) Just before serving coat each pear with the creamy mixture then sprinkle with the coconut.

Selections per serving: 1 Fruit, ½ Protein, 95 Optional Calories

TIP: *Don't spoon the fromage frais over the pears in advance or it will slip off the fruit.*

Festive Orange Slices ☆

Ingredients:

6 medium oranges
6fl oz (180ml) red wine
¼ teaspoon ground cinnamon
1oz (30g) sugar

Method:

1) Finely grate or remove the zest from 1 orange with a zester.

2) Place the orange zest together with the wine, cinnamon and sugar into a saucepan and bring to the boil over a low heat. Reduce the heat and simmer the mixture for 3-4 minutes.

3) Using a sharp knife slice the peel from all the oranges then cut them into thin slices.

4) Add the orange slices to the saucepan then cover the saucepan. Simmer the oranges for 4 minutes, carefully stirring twice during cooking.

5) Serve the Festive Oranges warm or chilled.

Selections per serving: 1½ Fruit, 70 Optional Calories

Gingery Bananas ☆

Ingredients:

1 tablespoon cornflour
½ teaspoon ground ginger
finely grated zest of ¼ lemon
6fl oz (180ml) skimmed milk
½ tablespoon golden syrup
1 teaspoon lemon juice
3 medium bananas

Method:

1) Place the cornflour, ginger and lemon zest in a small saucepan.

2) Gradually blend the milk into the cornflour mixture bring to the boil, stirring all the time, over a low heat. Boil for 2 minutes.

3) Remove the ginger sauce from the heat and stir in the golden syrup and lemon juice.

4) Peel the bananas and cut into small pieces. Stir the banana into the hot sauce and serve.

Selections per serving: 1½ Fruit, 30 Optional Calories

TIP: *Lightly oil the measuring spoon before spooning the golden syrup – this makes it easier to measure as the syrup slides off the spoon.*

Wholemeal Peach Flan ☆

Ingredients:

1 x 8 inch (20cm) cooked wholemeal pastry flan case
8oz (240g) well-drained canned peaches
4oz (120g) wholemeal self-raising flour
2oz (60g) margarine
2oz (60g) caster sugar
1 large egg
¼ teaspoon almond essence
1-2 tablespoons water or juice from the peaches
½ teaspoon icing sugar

Method:

1) Place the pastry case on a baking sheet.

2) Chop the drained peaches and arrange evenly over the flan.

3) Place the flour in a bowl, make a well in the centre and spoon the margarine and sugar into it.

4) Add the egg and almond essence to the bowl and mix all the ingredients together with a wooden spoon, add sufficient water or peach juice to give a smooth consistency which will drop easily from the spoon when tapped against the side of the bowl.

5) Using a teaspoon, spoon the mixture all over the flan and then spread so all the peaches are covered. Bake at 350F, 180C, Gas Mark 4 for 30-35 minutes.

6) Remove the flan from the oven and sieve the icing sugar over. Serve hot or cold.

Selections per serving: ¾ Bread, 1½ Fat, ¼ Fruit, 90 Optional Calories

Oaty Fruit ☆

Ingredients:

1½ tablespoons margarine
1 teaspoon honey
2oz (60g) porridge oats
3 medium bananas
6 fresh dates
½ teaspoon lemon juice

Method:

1) Spoon the margarine and honey into a saucepan and heat gently until the margarine has melted.

2) Stir the oats into the melted margarine and mix well so they are all coated with the margarine and honey.

3) Slice the bananas and place in a bowl.

4) Halve the dates, remove the stones and slide out of their skins. Cut each half in half again.

5) Mix the dates together with the bananas then stir in the lemon juice.

6) Spoon the fruit into four small ramekin dishes and sprinkle the oats over. Cook under a moderate grill until golden.

Selections per serving: ½ Bread, 1 Fat, 2 Fruit, 25 Optional Calories

TIP: *For a change substitute porridge oats with rye or barley flakes.*

Sweet Mixed Salad ☆

Ingredients:

10oz (300g) melon
1½ medium bananas
4 fresh dates
½ tablespoon caster sugar
2 teaspoons lemon juice
¼ teaspoon ground ginger

Method:

1) Cut the melon into 1 inch (2.5cm) cubes.

2) Slice the bananas.

3) Cut the dates in half and remove the stones. Cut each half lengthways in half.

4) Mix the prepared fruit together in a bowl.

5) Stir the sugar, lemon juice and ginger together then stir into the prepared fruits and leave to marinate for at least 1 hour. Stir the fruit and the syrup together before serving.

Selections per serving: 1¾ Fruit, 10 Optional Calories

Mandarin Custard☆

Ingredients:

finely grated zest of 1 medium orange
½oz (15g) cornflour
¼ pint (150ml) skimmed milk
6oz (180g) drained canned mandarins plus
    1 tablespoon of juice
½-1 teaspoon of lemon juice
artificial sweetener
1 tablespoon desiccated coconut

Method:

1) Place the orange zest zest in saucepan, add the cornflour and gradually blend in the milk.

2) Bring the sauce to the boil, stirring all the time. Boil for 2 minutes.

3) Stir the mandarins and the mandarin and lemon juice into the saucepan and bring to the boil, stirring all the time – don't worry if the mandarin segments break into small pieces. Sweeten to taste with artificial sweetener.

4) Spoon the mandarin sauce into three ramekins, sprinkle with the coconut and serve hot or leave until cold.

Selections per serving: ½ Fruit, 50 Optional Calories

TIP: *Serve the Orchard Pudding with a custard sauce.*

Orchard Pudding☆

Ingredients:

4oz (120g) fresh breadrumbs
½ teaspoon cinnamon
2 tablespoons caster sugar
3 medium cooking apples
1oz (30g) raisins or sultanas
2 tablespoons margarine

Method:

1) Mix the breadcrumbs, cinnamon and sugar together in a bowl.

2) Peel, quarter and core the apples. Roughly chop the apples then place in a bowl and mix together with the dried fruit.

3) Sprinkle half the breadcrumbs over the base of a deep 6½-7 inch (16.25-17.5cm) ovenproof dish.

4) Spread the fruit evenly over the breadcrumbs.

5) Melt the margarine over a low heat, add the breadcrumbs and stir round then remove from the heat and sprinkle over the apples and raisins.

6) Bake the Orchard Pudding at 325F, 180C, Gas Mark 4 for 30 minutes or until the apple is cooked and the breadcrumbs crisp and golden.

Selections per serving: 1 Bread, 1½ Fat, 1 Fruit, 30 Optional Calories

Fruity Cheese Starter ☆

Ingredients:

3oz (90g) small seedless black grapes
2 medium clementines
1 stick celery
2oz (60g) crumbly hard cheese,
   for example Caerphilly
a few lettuce leaves

Method:

1) Cut the grapes in half and place in a bowl.

2) Peel the clementines removing as much of the white membranes as possible then divide into segments.

3) Thinly slice the celery.

4) Mix the grapes together with the clementines and celery. Crumble the cheese into very small pieces and mix into the fruit and celery.

5) Arrange a little lettuce on four small serving plates then spoon the fruit and cheese mixture on top.

Selections per serving: ½ Fruit, ½ Protein, ¼ Vegetable

TIP: *To serve the Fruity Cheese Starter at a special celebration, use a combination of different coloured salad leaves.*

Prunes and Pears ☆

Ingredients:

4oz (120g) no-need-to-soak dried prunes
1 medium orange
2 tablespoons water
2 medium pears
½ tablespoon sugar

Method:

1) Place the prunes in a saucepan.

2) Peel a strip round the centre of the orange. Squeeze the juice from the orange and add it, together with the zest to the prunes.

3) Add the water then cover the saucepan and leave to simmer over a moderate heat for 10 minutes.

4) Peel, quarter then core the pears. Cut each quarter into three pieces.

5) Stir the sugar and chunks of pear into the prunes, cover the saucepan and leave to simmer for a further 6-10 minutes, depending on the firmness of the pears – if necessary add a little more water to the saucepan.

Selections per serving: 1½ Fruit, 25 Optional Calories

$\mathcal{V}$EGETABLES

Parsnip Gratin ☆

Ingredients:

12oz (360g) parsnips
salt
1oz (30g) cornflour
½ pint (300ml) skimmed milk
4oz (120g) fromage frais
2½oz (75g) Cheddar cheese

Method:

1) Thinly slice the parsnips, cook in boiling salted water for about 6 minutes until just cooked, drain well.

2) Blend the cornflour to a smooth paste with a little milk, gradually add the remaining milk to the mixture and bring to the boil, stirring all the time. Boil for 2 minutes then remove from the heat and stir in the fromage frais.

3) Reserve about ½oz (15g) cheese, add the remainder to the sauce and stir until it has melted.

4) Spread about half the slices of parsnip over the base of a flameproof dish, pour over about half the sauce then repeat the layers.

5) Sprinkle the reserved cheese over the Parsnip Gratin and cook under a hot grill until golden.

Selections per serving: 1 Bread, ¼ Milk, 1 Protein, 10 Optional Calories

TIP: Serve the Parsnip Gratin with a mixed salad to make an appetising lunch or supper dish.

Vegetable Salad ☆

Ingredients:

4oz (120g) carrots
4oz (120g) parsnips
4oz (120g) swede
4oz (120g) small cauliflower florets
salt
2oz (60g) curd cheese
2 tablespoons mayonnaise
4 tablespoons skimmed milk
2 teaspoons grated onion
paprika

Method:

1) Cut the carrots, parsnips and swede into 1 inch (2.5cm) thin lengths. Divide the cauliflower into very small florets.

2) Place the carrots and swede in a saucepan, cover with boiling water and add a little salt, boil for 4-5 minutes then add the cauliflower and parsnips and boil for a further 8-9 minutes until all the vegetables are cooked but still a little crisp.

3) Mix the curd cheese together with the mayonnaise, gradually blend in the milk, one spoonful at a time. Stir in the onion.

4) Drain the vegetables then cool under running cold water for 1 minute.

5) Stir the vegetables together with the curd cheese dressing then spoon into a serving bowl, sprinkle with paprika and serve.

Selections per serving: ¼ Bread, 1½ Fat, ¼ Protein, 1 Vegetable, 5 Optional Calories

Winter Salad ☆

Ingredients:

3 inch (7.5cm) slice of leek
4oz (120g) fennel
4oz (120g) carrot
1 medium apple
6 tablespoons low-fat natural yogurt
4 teaspoons mayonnaise

Method:

1) Slice the leek as thinly as possible then place it in a bowl.

2) Coarsely grate the fennel and carrot, add them to the leek.

3) Peel, quarter and core the apple then grate into the bowl.

4) Stir the yogurt and mayonnaise together then stir into the salad and mix well.

Selections per serving: 1 Fat, ¼ Fruit, ¾ Vegetable, 15 Optional Calories

TIP: *Serve the Creamy Broccoli Soup with a warm, crusty wholemeal roll on a chilly winter's day.*

Creamy Broccoli Soup ☆

Serves 4
105 Calories per serving

Ingredients:

4 teaspoons margarine
1 large onion, chopped
1lb (480g) calabrese broccoli
finely grated zest of ½ lemon
½ pint (300ml) vegetable stock
8fl oz (240ml) skimmed milk
juice of 1 lemon
salt and pepper
2 tablespoons single cream

Method:

1) Melt 2 teaspoons margarine in a saucepan, add the onion and stir over a moderate heat for 1-2 minutes. Cover the pan and leave over a low heat for 6-7 minutes.

2) Roughly chop the broccoli.

3) Add the remaining margarine to the saucepan, stir round then add the chopped broccoli. Continue stirring for 1-2 minutes then cover and leave over a low heat for 5 minutes.

4) Add the lemon zest and stock to the broccoli, cover and leave to simmer 20-25 minutes.

5) Pour the broccoli and stock into a liquidiser or food processor and process to a purée.

6) Pour the purée into the saucepan, stir in the milk and gradually add the lemon juice – taste the soup when you have added about three-quarters of the juice then continue adding to suit your taste.

7) Season the soup with salt and pepper then reheat, stirring all the time.

8) Pour the soup into four bowls and swirl the cream into each serving.

Selections per serving: 1 Fat, 2 Vegetable, 45 Optional Calories

Parsnip Curry ☆

Ingredients:

1 small clove garlic
½ medium onion
½ medium cooking apple
1lb (480g) parsnips
2 teaspoons oil
1 teaspoon finely chopped ginger
½ tablespoon flour
3-4 teaspoons Madras curry powder
1 tablespoon tomato purée
4 teaspoons desiccated coconut
8fl oz (240ml) stock or water
salt
lemon juice

Method:

1) Finely chop the garlic. Chop the onion and apple and cut the parsnips into 1 inch (2.5cm) cubes.

2) Heat the oil in a saucepan, add the garlic and ginger and stir-fry for 1-2 minutes. Add the onion and stir-fry for 3-4 minutes.

3) Sprinkle the flour and curry powder into the saucepan and stir well then add the chopped apple, tomato purée, coconut, stock or water and parsnips.

4) Bring to the boil, stirring all the time then cover the saucepan and leave to simmer for 20-25 minutes until the parsnips are cooked.

5) Season to taste with a little salt and lemon juice.

Selections per serving: 2 Bread, 1 Fat, ¼ Fruit, ¼ Vegetable, 30 Optional Calories

TIP: Brush the remaining half apple from the curry with a little lemon juice and store in the refrigerator for use the next day.

Saucy Onions ☆

Ingredients:

1lb (480g) onions
1 tablespoon margarine
3 tablespoons water or vegetable stock
4 teaspoons cornflour
7fl oz (210ml) skimmed milk
salt and pepper

Method:

1) Thinly slice the onions.

2) Melt the margarine in a saucepan, add the onions and stir round then cover and leave over a low heat for 10 minutes.

3) Stir the water or stock into the onion slices, cover the saucepan and cook over a moderate heat for 15-20 minutes, stirring once or twice during the cooking time, until just cooked.

4) Blend the cornflour together with the milk.

5) Stir the cornflour and milk into the saucepan. Cook over a moderate heat for 3 minutes, stirring all the time. Season generously with salt and pepper then serve.

Selections per serving: ¾ Fat, 1¼ Vegetable, 25 Optional Calories

Mushroom Topping ☆

Ingredients:

6oz (180g) mushrooms
½ small onion
1 teaspoon margarine
½ teaspoon ground coriander
½oz (15g) cornflour
¼ pint (150ml) skimmed milk
3 tablespoons soured cream
salt and pepper

Method:

1) Chop the mushrooms. Finely chop the onion.

2) Melt the margarine in a saucepan, add the onion and stir-fry for 3 minutes.

3) Stir the coriander and chopped mushrooms into the saucepan, cover and leave over a low heat for 3 minutes.

4) Stir the mushrooms well, increase the heat and continue stirring for about 3 minutes until the mushroom liquid has evaporated.

5) Blend the cornflour with the milk then pour into the saucepan and bring to the boil, stirring all the time. Boil for 2 minutes then remove from the heat, add the soured cream and season to taste with salt and pepper. Serve as a topping on jacket potatoes or pasta.

Selections per serving: ¼ Bread, ½ Fat, ¼ Milk, 1¼ Vegetable, 75 Optional Calories

---

TIP: *Keep a supply of canned vegetables in the store cupboard. They make interesting additions to many dishes.*

Canny Casserole ☆

Ingredients:

1 x 480g can baby corn on the cob
1 x 432g can chick peas
1 x 297g can whole carrots
1 x 300g can whole button mushrooms
1 x 400g can chopped tomatoes
3 tablespoons dried red and green peppers
½ tablespoon onion powder
¼ teaspoon mixed herbs
4 tablespoons water
¼ teaspoon yeast extract

Method:

1) Drain the cans of baby corn, chick peas, carrots and mushrooms.

2) Place the chopped tomatoes in a saucepan, add the peppers together with the onion powder, mixed herbs, water and yeast extract. Stir all the ingredients together well.

3) Stir the drained vegetables into the tomato mixture.

4) Heat the mixture over a moderate heat, stir well then cover the saucepan and leave to simmer for 12 minutes, stirring twice during the cooking time.

5) Ladle the Canny Casserole into a warm serving dish.

Selections per serving: ¾ Bread, ¾ Protein, 2½ Vegetable

Orange Root Mix ☆

Ingredients:

9oz (270g) mixture of carrots, swede and turnips
salt
1½ teaspoons orange and ginger sauce
3 tablespoons low-fat natural yogurt
1 teaspoon finely chopped spring onion

Method:

1) Cut the carrots, swede and turnips into 1½ inch (4cm) long sticks.

2) Cook the prepared vegetables in boiling salted water until cooked but still a little crisp.

4) Stir the orange and ginger sauce into the yogurt.

5) Drain the vegetables and stir them into the yogurt sauce, transfer to a serving dish and sprinkle with the spring onions.

Selections per serving: 1½ Vegetable, 25 Optional Calories

TIP: *Substitute some of the Orange Root Mix vegetables with parsnips but alter the Selections as necessary.*

German Kale

Ingredients:

8oz (240g) kale, tough stalks removed
1 small onion
1½ teaspoons olive oil
4oz (120g) frankfurters
3 tablespoons wine vinegar
¼ teaspoon German or Dijon mustard
salt and pepper

Method:

1) Wash the kale. Cut or tear any large leaves into two or three pieces.

2) Place the kale and a little water in a saucepan and boil for 6 minutes until bright green and almost cooked.

3) Finely chop the onion. Heat the oil in a saucepan, add the onion and stir-fry over a low heat for 1 minute then cover the saucepan and leave over a very low heat for 4-5 minutes until the onion is soft.

4) While the onion is cooking, cook the frankfurters according to the packaging instructions.

5) Drain the kale and cut the frankfurters into ½ inch (1.25cm) thick slices.

6) Whisk the vinegar together with the mustard and a little salt and pepper.

7) Stir the kale, frankfurters and vinegar into the onion and cook over a low heat for about 4 minutes, stirring all the time, until the kale is cooked.

Selections per serving: ¾ Fat, 1½ Protein, 1½ Vegetable

Mixed Cabbage Salad ☆

Serves 4
90 Calories per serving

Ingredients:

¼ small red cabbage – about 6oz (180g)
¼ small white cabbage about 6oz (180g)
1-2 teaspoons lemon juice
5fl oz (150ml) very low-fat banana yogurt
2oz (60g) Danish blue cheese

Method:

1) Finely shred the red and white cabbages, cutting across the width of each cabbage. Discard the hard central core.

2) Place the cabbage in a saucepan, add 1 teaspoon lemon juice and cover with boiling water. Cover the saucepan and boil over a moderate heat for 5 minutes until the cabbage is still crisp but a little limp. Drain the cabbage and transfer to a bowl.

3) Stir the yogurt into the hot cabbage.

4) Cut the cheese into small dice and stir into the cabbage together with a little more lemon juice. Leave until cold then serve with a selection of other salads.

Selections per serving: ½ Protein, 1 Vegetable, 25 Optional Calories

TIP: *Use the breadcrumb topping from the Carrot Gratin to liven up other vegetable purées.*

Carrot Gratin ☆

Serves 4
105 Calories per serving

Ingredients:

1lb (480g) carrots
salt
4oz (120g) fromage frais
pepper
1 tablespoon margarine
1oz (30g) fresh breadcrumbs
1 tablespoon finely grated Parmesan cheese

Method:

1) Halve small young carrots or cut larger carrots into thick slices. Reserve 2-3oz (60-90g) carrots and cut them into very small dice.

2) Place the large pieces of carrot in a saucepan, cover with boiling water and add a little salt. Bring to the boil and cook for 12 minutes then add the diced carrots and cook for a further 3-4 minutes.

3) Drain the carrots and transfer the large pieces to a liquidiser. Add the fromage frais and process to a purée.

4) Stir the diced carrot into the purée and season to taste with salt and pepper then spoon into a shallow flameproof dish.

5) Melt the margarine in a small saucepan, add the breadcrumbs and stir to cover all the crumbs with the margarine. Remove from the heat and stir in the Parmesan cheese.

6) Sprinkle the breadcrumb and cheese mixture over the carrot purée and brown under a hot grill.

Selections per serving: ¼ Bread, ¾ Fat, ½ Protein, 1¼ Vegetable, 10 Optional Calories

Parsnip Purée ☆

Ingredients:

1lb 4oz (600g) parsnips
salt
4oz (120g) cooking apple, peeled and cored
2oz (60g) fromage frais

Method:

1) Cut the parsnips into chunks then cook in boiling salted water.

2) Chop the apple and place in a very small saucepan, add 1 tablespoon water and cover the saucepan. Place over a very low heat and leave to cook slowly for 4 minutes. Leave the saucepan for 2-3 minutes to allow the apple to cook completely.

3) Drain the parsnips and mash well until smooth. Add the apple and its cooking liquid and mash once again.

4) Beat the fromage frais into the parsnip and apple then season to taste with a little salt.

Selections per serving: 1¼ Bread, ¼ Fruit, ¼ Protein,

TIP: *Serve these vegetables as accompaniments to main meal dishes.*

Creamy Potatoes ☆

Ingredients:

1lb 8oz (720g) potatoes
2 onions
2 tablespoons margarine
2 tablespoons grated Parmesan cheese
salt and pepper
4fl oz (120ml) skimmed milk
4 tablespoons double cream

Method:

1) Slice the potatoes as thinly as possible.

2) Thinly slice the onions.

3) Melt 1 tablespoon margarine in a saucepan, add the onions and stir-fry for 2-3 minutes then cover the saucepan and leave over a low heat for 6-7 minutes until cooked.

4) Lay about a third of potatoes in an ovenproof dish, cover with half the onions then top with half the remaining potatoes.

5) Sprinkle the potatoes in the dish with 1 tablespoon cheese and a little salt and pepper. Spread the remaining onions over then top with a layer of potato slices. Dot with the remaining margarine.

6) Cover the dish with foil and cook at 350C, 180C, Gas Mark 4 for 45 minutes. Stir the milk and cream together then pour over the potatoes and sprinkle over the remaining cheese. Return to the oven and cook for a further 45 minutes until cooked.

Selections per serving: 1¼ Bread, 1 Fat, ¼ Vegetable
55 Optional Calories

Snow White Salad ☆

Ingredients:

¼ small white cabbage – about 6oz (180g)
2 large sticks celery
1 medium apple
1½ tablespoons mayonnaise
4oz (120g) cottage cheese
1 teaspoon lemon juice

Method:

1) Finely shred the white cabbage, cutting across the width of the cabbage. Discard the hard central core.

2) Finely chop the celery. Finely chop any celery leaves but set aside, do not add to the other ingredients.

3) Peel, quarter and core the apple then chop finely.

4) Stir the cabbage together with the celery and apple.

5) Spoon the mayonnaise into a small bowl. Sieve the cottage cheese into the mayonnaise and mix together with 1 teaspoon lemon juice.

6) Stir the cottage cheese mixture evenly through the cabbage, celery and apple. Spoon the salad into a serving bowl and scatter the chopped celery leaves over.

Selection per serving: 1 Fat, ¼ Fruit, ½ Protein, ¾ Vegetable, 5 Optional Calories

---

TIP: *If you are unable to buy fresh dill for the Buttered Artichokes, substitute with fresh chervil.*

Buttered Artichokes ☆

Ingredients:

1lb (480g) Jerusalem artichokes
lemon juice
salt
2 teaspoons butter
½ tablespoon finely chopped dill
black pepper

Method:

1) Scrub and thinly peel the artichokes – don't worry if some skin remains attached, it is similar to the skin on new potatoes.

2) Thickly slice the artichokes and place in a saucepan. Cover the artichokes with boiling water, add 1 teaspoon lemon juice and a little salt and cover the saucepan. Cook for 6-8 minutes until tender then drain.

3) Mash the butter then mix in the dill and a little black pepper and lemon juice.

4) Add the herb butter to the hot drained artichokes and toss to coat all the slices, if desired add a little more lemon juice.

Selections per serving: 1½ Vegetable, 15 Optional Calories

Red Cabbage Salad ☆

Ingredients:

10oz (300g) red cabbage, central core removed
1 red onion
1 medium red dessert apple, cored
4 tablespoons red wine vinegar
4 teaspoons olive oil
2 cloves garlic, crushed
good pinch of powdered mustard
¼ teaspoon mixed herbs
salt and pepper

Method:

1) Finely shred the red cabbage, grate the onion and apple. The simplest way of doing this preparation is by using a food processor fitted with a grating attachment.

2) Place the vinegar, oil, garlic, mustard, herbs and a sprinkling of salt and pepper in a screw-top jar, secure and shake well. Alternatively place all the ingredients in a small bowl and whisk well to mix.

3) Pour the dressing over the salad, stir well to thoroughly coat the cabbage, onion and apple. Transfer to a non-metallic bowl, cover and leave in a cool place for 3-4 hours.

4) Before serving stir and add extra seasoning if necessary.

Selections per serving: 1 Fat, ¼ Fruit, 1 Vegetable

TIP: *A Gala or Red Delicious apple is ideal for the Red Cabbage Salad.*

Marbled Vegetables ☆

Ingredients:

12oz (360g) Brussels sprouts
1lb 2oz (540g) potatoes
salt
4oz (120g) fromage frais
lemon juice
pepper
2 teaspoons margarine

Method:

1) Cut a cross in the base of each Brussels sprout, cut the potatoes into chunks. Place the sprouts and potatoes in separate saucepans, cover with boiling water and add a little salt. Boil until completely cooked.

2) Drain the hot vegetables. Place the Brussels sprouts in a food processor, add half the fromage frais and process to a purée. Season to taste with a little lemon juice, salt and pepper.

3) Mash the potatoes with the margarine, add the remaining fromage frais and mix well. Season to taste with salt and pepper.

4) Place spoonfuls of the Brussels sprouts purée unevenly into an ovenproof dish, add spoonfuls of potato into the dish and swirl the two purées together with a fork. Roughen the surface and place in a hot oven 375F, 190C, Gas Mark 5 for 10 minutes.

Selections per serving: 1½ Bread, ½ Fat, ½ Protein, 1 Vegetable

Artichoke Salad

Ingredients:

1lb (480g) Jerusalem artichokes
2-3 teaspoons lemon juice
1½oz (45g) lean smoked back bacon
8 tablespoons low-fat natural yogurt
1 teaspoon Dijon mustard
1½oz (45g) gherkins

Method:

1) Slice the artichokes and place in a saucepan, cover with boiling water and add 2 teaspoons lemon juice. Boil for about 12 minutes until cooked.

2) Derind the bacon then lay on the rack of a grill pan and cook, turning once, until cooked and beginning to crisp. Allow to cool then cut into small pieces.

3) Mix the yogurt together with the mustard and add a little lemon juice to taste.

4) Rinse the gherkins under running cold water then slice thinly.

5) Drain the artichokes then mix them together with the gherkins and yogurt dressing. Leave to cool.

Selections per serving: ¾ Protein, 1¼ Vegetable, 20 Optional Calories

TIP: *Roast vegetables are tasty accompanyments to hot or cold dishes.*

Roasted Potatoes and Parsnips☆

Ingredients:

1lb 4oz (600g) potatoes
1lb (480g) parsnips
1½ tablespoons oil
½ tablespoon margarine
salt

Method:

1) Peel the potatoes and parsnips.

2) Leave the potatoes whole if small otherwise cut into large chunks.

3) Spoon the oil into a baking tin just large enough to hold all the vegetables without touching. Place the baking tin in a preheated oven, 425F, 210C, Gas Mark 7, leave in the oven for 5 minutes until the oil is extremely hot.

4) Add the margarine and swirl round so it melts then add the vegetables. Turn the potatoes and parsnips in the hot fat then sprinkle with salt and return to the oven. Cook at 400-425F, 200-210C, Gas Mark 6-7 for 1 hour 15 minutes or until golden and cooked.

Selections per serving: 2½ Bread, 1½ Fat, 15 Optional Calories

Winter Soup ✩

Ingredients:

3oz (90g) swede
3oz (90g) turnip
3oz (90g) carrot
3oz (90g) celeriac
3oz (90g) potato
4oz (120g) parsnip
1 medium onion
1 teaspoon oil
8oz (240g) can tomatoes
1oz (30g) split red lentils
¼-½ teaspoon chilli powder
¼ teaspoon oregano
¾ pint (450ml) vegetable stock
4oz (120g) Brussels sprouts

Method:

1) Cut the swede, turnip, carrot, celeriac, potato and parsnip into ¾ inch (2cm) chunks. Roughly chop the onion.

2) Heat the oil in a saucepan, add the onion and stir round for 1 minute. Cover and leave over a very low heat for 4-5 minutes.

3) Add all the prepared vegetables, tomatoes, lentils, chilli powder, oregano and stock. Cover and simmer for 20 minutes.

4) Cut the Brussels sprouts in half, or if very large in quarters, then add to the saucepan, cover and simmer for 10-12 minutes until all the vegetables are cooked.

Selections per serving: ½ Bread, ¼ Fat, ¼ Protein, 2½ Vegetable

---

TIP: *Choose good quality firm root vegetables. Don't purchase any that are soft. They may be cheaper but they lack flavour and texture.*

Braised Vegetables ✩

Ingredients:

3 leeks
1lb 8oz (720g) mixture turnips, swede, carrots and celery
1 tablespoon oil
½ tablespoon tomato purée
7fl oz (210ml) stock
1 bay leaf
¼ teaspoon mixed herbs
salt and pepper

Method:

1) Cut the leeks into 3 inch (7.5cm) lengths and leave to soak while preparing the other vegetables – this will help to remove the grit between the layers of leek, but if they are very dirty split them in half lengthways.

2) Leave very small turnips whole but cut large ones and the swede into 1½ inch (4cm) cubes.

3) Cut the carrots in half or if very large into three or four pieces.

4) Cut the celery into 3 inch (7.5cm) lengths, chop any leaves.

5) Heat the oil in a flameproof casserole, add the leeks and stir-fry for 4-5 minutes until just beginning to brown. Add the other vegetables to the casserole.

6) Stir the tomato purée together with the stock then add the herbs and a little salt and pepper. Pour the stock mixture over the vegetables and bring to the boil. Cover the casserole then transfer to a preheated oven and cook at 325F, 160C, Gas Mark 3 for 2 hours or until the vegetables are cooked.

Selections per serving: ¾ Fat, 3 Vegetable, 5 Optional Calories

Winter Soup

Brussels Soufflé (See page 38)

DAIRY

Brussels Soufflé ☆

Ingredients:

8oz (240g) Brussels sprouts (prepared weight, approximately 10oz (300g) purchased weight)
1½ tablespoons margarine
1oz (30g) flour
¼ pint (150ml) skimmed milk
2oz (60g) hard cheese, finely grated
3 eggs, separated
1 egg white
pinch of cream of tartar
½ tablespoon grated Parmesan cheese

Method:

1) Prepare the Brussels sprouts: Remove any coarse outer leaves, make two cuts in the base of each sprout, cutting through the centre in a cross. Boil or steam the Brussels sprouts, drain well.

2) Grease a 7 inch (17.5cm) soufflé dish with a little of the margarine. Melt the remainder in a saucepan, add the flour and stir round, then remove from the heat and gradually add the milk. Return to the heat and bring to the boil, stirring all the time. Add the grated hard cheese and stir until melted.

3) Transfer the cooked and well-drained Brussels sprouts to a liquidiser or food processor, add the cheese sauce and process. Add the egg yolks to the liquidiser and process once again then pour the purée into a large bowl.

4) Whisk the four egg whites with a pinch of cream of tartar until peaking. Using a metal spoon carefully fold the egg white into the purée.

5) Spoon the mixture into the greased soufflé dish, sprinkle over the Parmesan cheese and bake at 350F, 180C, Gas Mark 4 for about 40 minutes until golden and well-risen. Serve immediately.

Selections per serving: ¼ Bread, ¼ Fat, 1¼ Protein, ¾ Vegetable, 25 Optional Calories

TIP: *Always make guests wait for a soufflé not the soufflé wait for the guests!*

Osbourne Pudding ☆

Ingredients:

4 x 1oz (30g) thin slices bread
2 tablespoons margarine
3 tablespoons marmalade
3oz (90g) mixture raisins and sultanas
2 eggs
½ pint (300ml) skimmed milk

Method:

1) Spread the bread with the margarine and then the marmalade. Cut each slice into four triangles.

2) Arrange one third of the bread in a pie dish, sprinkle over half the dried fruit. Repeat these layers then cover with the remaining triangles of bread.

3) Whisk the eggs and milk together then pour over the layered pudding and leave for 20-30 minutes to allow the milk to soak into the bread.

4) Bake the Osbourne Pudding at 350F, 180C, Gas Mark 4 for 35-40 minutes until golden brown and puffy.

Selections per serving: 1 Bread, 1½ Fat, ¾ Fruit, ¼ Milk, ½ Protein, 40 Optional Calories

Bulgar Savoury ☆

Serves 4
215 Calories per serving

Ingredients:

½ medium onion
½ green pepper
2 teaspoons olive oil
6oz (180g) bulgar wheat
12fl oz (360ml) boiling water or weak stock
2oz (60g) gherkins
10 small olives, stoned
4oz (120g) cottage cheese
salt and pepper

Method:

1) Finely chop the onion and green pepper.

2) Gently heat the oil in a saucepan, add the onion and stir-fry for 2-3 minutes. Add the green pepper and stir-fry for 4 minutes.

3) Stir the bulgar wheat and the boiling water or stock into the onion mixture. Cover the saucepan and leave over a low heat for 6 minutes.

4) Thinly slice the gherkins and finely chop the olives.

5) Stir the gherkins, olives and cottage cheese into the hot bulgar wheat mixture. Stir the mixture over a low heat for 1-2 minutes then season with salt and pepper and serve.

Selections per serving: 1½ Bread, ¾ Fat, ½ Protein, ½ Vegetable

TIP: *Use bulgar wheat in place of all or some of the rice in salads.*

Cheddar Pudding

Serves 4
300 Calories per serving

Ingredients:

1oz (30g) rasher lean smoked back bacon, derinded
2 tablespoons margarine
1 tablespoon grated onion
4 x 1oz (30g) slices bread
3oz (90g) mature Cheddar cheese, grated
2 eggs
½ pint (300ml) skimmed milk
salt and pepper

Method:

1) Lay the bacon on the rack of a grill pan and cook, turning once, until cooked but not crisp. Chop into very small pieces.

2) Spoon the margarine into a small bowl, add the grated onion and mash into the margarine. Spread the slices of bread with the margarine mixture then cut each slice into four squares.

3) Lay five squares of bread, margarine side uppermost in a pie dish, sprinkle over half the bacon and about one third of the cheese. Repeat these layers.

4) Arrange the remaining six squares of bread, margarine side uppermost on top then sprinkle over the remaining cheese.

5) Whisk the eggs together with the milk, season with a little salt and pepper then pour the mixture over the pudding and set aside for 15-20 minutes. Bake at 350F, 180C, Gas Mark 4 for 35-40 minutes until well-risen, golden and puffy, serve immediately.

Selections per serving: 1 Bread, 1½ Fat, ¼ Milk, 1¾ Protein

Broccoli Flan ☆

Ingredients:

12oz (360g) calabrese broccoli
salt
6oz (180g) cottage cheese
pepper
3 eggs
8 inch (20cm) cooked flan case

Method:

1) Cook the broccoli in boiling salted water. Drain well and place in a liquidiser or food processor, add the cottage cheese and process.

2) Add the eggs to the broccoli and cheese and process once again. Season with salt and pepper.

3) Pour the broccoli and cheese purée into the flan case and bake at 350F, 180C, Gas Mark 4 for about 35 minutes or until risen and firm to touch.

4) Cut into wedges and serve hot with vegetables or leave until cool and serve with a salad.

Selections per serving: ½ Bread, ¾ Protein, ½ Vegetable, 50 Optional Calories

TIP: *To obtain a crisp pastry base, place the baking sheet containing the flan directly on top of a hot baking sheet which has been in the preheated oven.*

Pasta Supper

Ingredients:

1 egg
salt
3oz (90g) pasta bows or spirals
1 tablespoon margarine
½ medium onion, finely chopped
½ red pepper, finely chopped
4 tablespoons soured cream
4 tablespoons skimmed milk
pepper sauce
4oz (120g) peeled prawns
lemon juice (optional)

Method:

1) Place the egg in a saucepan, cover with cold water and add about ½ teaspoon salt. Place the saucepan over a moderate heat and bring to the boil. Boil for 10 minutes then drain, cool the egg under running cold water and remove the shell. Chop finely.

2) Cook the pasta in slightly salted boiling water.

3) Melt the margarine in a saucepan, add the onion and stir-fry for 4 minutes, add the red pepper, stir round then cover the saucepan and leave over a low heat for 3-4 minutes.

4) Stir the soured cream and milk together then add a dash of pepper sauce.

5) Stir the hot pasta and prawns into the hot onion and red pepper. Add the soured cream mixture and chopped egg and stir over a low heat until the Pasta Supper is very hot. Remove from the heat and add more pepper sauce or lemon juice to taste.

Selections per serving: 1½ Bread, 1½ Fat, 2½ Protein, ¾ Vegetable, 110 Optional Calories

Creamed Rice with Fruit☆

Ingredients:

½oz (15g) powdered skimmed milk
¾oz (20g) ground rice
½ pint (300ml) skimmed milk
1 tablespoon frozen concentrated orange juice
1oz (30g) sultanas
artificial sweetener

Method:

1) Mix the powdered milk and ground rice together in a bowl.

2) Gradually mix the liquid milk into the bowl then pour into a small saucepan.

3) Bring the ground rice and milk to the boil, stirring all the time. Continue stirring and simmer the milk pudding for 7-8 minutes.

4) Stir the orange juice and sultanas into the simmering milk pudding, stir well and continue cooking for 3-4 minutes.

5) Remove the saucepan from the heat and sweeten to taste with artificial sweetener.

Selections per serving: ¼ Bread, ¾ Fruit, ¾ Milk, 10 Optional Calories

TIP: *Keep a carton of frozen orange juice in the freezer. It can be used to add a "tang" to drinks and desserts.*

Cauliflower Cheese Soup☆

Ingredients:

1 onion
1 cauliflower (approximately 1lb (480g) trimmed weight)
1 teaspoon margarine
8fl oz (240ml) stock
1 tablespoon cornflour
½ pint (300ml) skimmed milk
1½ teaspoons Dijon mustard
3oz (90g) hard cheese, grated
salt and pepper

Method:

1) Chop the onion and cauliflower.

2) Heat the margarine in a saucepan, add the onion and stir-fry for 3-4 minutes.

3) Add the cauliflower and stock to the onion, bring to the boil over a gentle heat, cover and leave to simmer for about 15 to 20 minutes or until the cauliflower is soft.

4) While the cauliflower is cooking make the cheese sauce: Blend the cornflour with the milk. Bring to the boil stirring all the time. Remove from the heat and add the mustard and cheese, stir round until the cheese has melted.

5) Pour the cauliflower and stock into a food processor or liquidiser, process to a purée. Add the cheese sauce and process once again. Reheat the soup over a low heat, stirring continuously, add salt and pepper to taste.

Selections per serving: ¼ Fat, ¼ Milk, ¾ Protein, 1¾ Vegetable, 10 Optional Calories

Rice Flan☆

Ingredients:

1 pint (600ml) skimmed milk
finely grated zest of ¼ lemon
2 tablespoons frozen concentrated orange juice,
*   thawed*
4oz (120g) ground rice
2 tablespoons sugar
1 x 8 inch (20cm) cooked pastry flan case
6oz (180g) drained canned mandarins

Method:

1) Reserve 5-6 tablespoons milk, place the remainder in a small saucepan, add the lemon zest and orange juice and heat until steaming.

2) Stir the remaining milk into the ground rice and then stir the mixture into the steaming milk. Bring to the boil, stirring all the time, reduce the heat as low as possible and continue cooking for about 10 minutes until the mixture is cooked and extremely thick.

3) Sweeten the mixture with the sugar then spoon into the flan case and level the surface. Leave to cool.

4) Just before serving, arrange the mandarin segments on top of the flan.

Selections per serving: 1 Bread, ¼ Fruit, ¼ Milk, 70 Optional Calories

---

TIP: *For an attractive accompaniment, pipe the potatoes into little flat basket shapes then, when cooked, fill with tiny cooked and diced carrots.*

Piped Potatoes☆

Ingredients:

12oz (360g) potatoes
salt
2oz (60g) Gorgonzola cheese
1 egg yolk
¼ teaspoon mustard
1½-2 tablespoons skimmed milk
½ teaspoon oil

Method:

1) Cut the potatoes into chunks and cook in boiling salted water then drain well.

2) Grate or crumble the cheese into small pieces.

3) Sieve the hot potatoes or mash until completely smooth. Beat in the cheese.

4) Mix the egg yolk, mustard and 1 tablespoon of milk together then beat into the mashed cheese potato. If necessary add a little more milk to give a creamy consistency.

5) Brush a large baking sheet with the oil then spoon the smooth mashed potato into a piping bag fitted with a ½ inch (1.25cm) fluted nozzle.

6) Pipe the potato mixture in rosettes. Brown the rosettes under a hot grill or place in a hot oven 400F, 200C, Gas Mark 6 for 12-15 minutes.

Selections per serving: 1 Bread, ½ Protein, 20 Optional Calories

Chocolate and Vanilla Dessert

Ingredients:

2oz (60g) cornflour
2 tablespoons cocoa
1 pint (600ml) skimmed milk
8 teaspoons sugar
few drops vanilla essence
2 teaspoons gelatine

Method:

1) Place 1oz (30g) cornflour in a small saucepan. Add the cocoa and gradually blend in ½ pint (300ml) milk. Bring to the boil, stirring all the time, boil for 2 minutes.

2) Pour the chocolate sauce into a bowl, stir in half the sugar and leave to cool.

3) Spoon the remaining cornflour into a small saucepan then gradually blend in the remaining milk. Add the vanilla essence and bring to the boil, stirring all the time, boil for 2 minutes.

4) Pour the white sauce into a bowl add the remaining sugar and leave to cool.

5) Place 2 tablespoons hot water in a small bowl or cup, sprinkle in the gelatine and stand in a saucepan of simmering water until the gelatine has completely dissolved.

6) Stir 1 tablespoon of the gelatine liquid into the chocolate sauce then stir the remainder into the white sauce. Leave to cool, stirring occasionally to prevent a skin forming.

7) When the sauces are cool and beginning to set, gently stir the white sauce unevenly into the chocolate sauce, then spoon into 4 serving glasses. If you prefer, spoon the sauces alternately into each glass. Chill until set.

Selections per serving: ½ Bread, ½ Milk, 55 Optional Calories

---

TIP: *Use vegetable based setting agent for the Chocolate and Vanilla Dessert when serving vegetarians.*

Avocado Dip ☆

Ingredients:

½ medium avocado
1 tablespoon lemon juice
4 teaspoons chopped chives
2oz (60g) cottage cheese
4oz (120g) curd cheese
salt
dash of pepper sauce
lemon slices

Method:

1) Scoop the avocado flesh into a blender, scraping the skin to obtain the light green colour.

2) Add the lemon juice, chives and cottage and curd cheeses; process until smooth. Season to taste with salt and pepper sauce.

3) Spoon the Avocado Dip into a small serving bowl and garnish with lemon slices.

Selections per serving: 1 Fat, ¾ Protein

Panlete

Ingredients:

½oz (15g) rasher lean smoked back bacon,
   derinded
2oz (60g) cottage cheese
1 egg
1 tablespoon flour
salt and pepper
½ tablespoon oil

Method:

1) Lay the bacon on the rack of a grill pan and cook, turning once until beginning to crisp, then chop into small pieces.

2) Place the cottage cheese, egg and flour in a liquidiser and process. Add the bacon and a little salt and pepper and process once again.

3) Heat the oil in a small frying pan. When the oil is very hot pour in the batter and cook over a moderate heat until the base is a dark golden colour. Transfer the frying pan to a hot grill and cook for about a minute until the Panlete is completely set.

4) Fold the Panlete in half and slide onto a warm plate.

Selections per serving: 1½ Fat, 3 Protein, 30 Optional Calories

TIP: *The Mushroom Dip may be spooned onto hot baked potatoes and accompanied by a mixed salad to make a light lunch or supper.*

Mushroom Dip ☆

Ingredients:

1 small onion
6oz (180g) cap or flat mushrooms
1 tablespoon sesame oil
4oz (120g) cottage cheese

Method:

1) Finely chop the onion. Chop the mushrooms.

2) Heat half the oil in a saucepan, add the onion and stir-fry for 1-2 minutes. Cover the saucepan and leave over a low heat for 5 minutes.

3) Add the remaining oil and mushrooms stir round for 1-2 minutes then cover the saucepan and leave over a low heat for 6 minutes, stirring once or twice during the cooking time.

4) Remove the lid from the saucepan and increase the heat. Continue cooking the mushroom mixture, stirring all the time, until only a little of the liquid remains – no more than 2-3 teaspoons.

5) Allow the mushroom mixture to cool a little then transfer to the goblet of a liquidiser and process to a purée. Add the cottage cheese and process once again.

6) Spoon the mushroom purée into a small bowl and leave until cool. Stir the dip before serving.

Selections per serving: ¾ Fat, ½ Protein, ¾ Vegetable

Puffy Semolina Pudding ☆

Serves 4
165 Calories per serving

Ingredients:

1 pint (600ml) skimmed milk
2oz (60g) semolina
¼ teaspoon ground cinnamon
1½ tablespoons sugar
2 eggs, separated
pinch of cream of tartar

Method:

1) Mix 3 tablespoons milk together with the semolina, pour the remainder into a saucepan.

2) Heat the milk until steaming then pour in the semolina mixture and cinnamon. Bring to the boil, stirring all the time, then simmer for about 10 minutes, stirring frequently until thick.

3) Remove the semolina from the heat and stir in the sugar and egg yolks.

4) Whisk the egg whites with the cream of tartar until peaking.

5) Gently fold the egg whites into the hot semolina then spoon into an ovenproof dish and bake at 350F, 180C, Gas Mark 4 for 40 minutes until well-risen and a light golden colour.

Selections per serving: ½ Bread, ½ Milk, ½ Protein, 20 Optional Calories

TIP: *If preferred, substitute semolina with the same quantity of ground rice.*

Pancakes ☆

Serves 4
180 Calories per serving

Ingredients:

4oz (120g) plain flour
salt
1 egg
½ pint (300ml) skimmed milk
1 tablespoon oil

Method:

1) Sieve the flour and a pinch of salt into a bowl, make a well in the centre, add the egg and gradually beat or whisk in the milk, set aside.

2) Prove a 7 inch (18cm) frying pan. Generously sprinkle salt all over the base of the frying pan, heat gently, tip out the salt then wipe thoroughly with a pad of kitchen paper. Heat a small amount of oil in the pan and wipe round the pan again.

3) Heat a little oil in the pan. Stir the batter then pour a little into the hot pan whilst turning to thinly coat the base. Cook over a moderate heat until the underside is golden, turn or toss over and cook the other side.

4) Transfer the cooked pancake to a plate, cover and keep warm in a low oven whilst repeating the procedure until all the batter has been cooked. This quantity will make 14-16 pancakes.

Selections per serving: 1 Bread, ¾ Fat, ¼ Milk, ¼ Protein

Custard Sauce ☆

Ingredients:

2 tablespoons custard powder
1 pint (600ml) skimmed milk
1 tablespoon sugar

(For Christmas Dinner for 6 or 8 add half, or double ingredients accordingly)

Method:

1) Place the custard powder in a bowl.

2) Gradually blend about 3 tablespoons milk into the custard powder to make a smooth paste.

3) Pour the remaining milk into a small saucepan and heat until steaming.

3) Pour the hot milk onto the custard powder mixture, stirring all the time.

4) Pour the custard powder mixture back into the saucepan, add the sugar and bring to the boil stirring all the time. Boil for 2 minutes. Serve hot or cold with fruit.

Selections per serving: ½ Milk, 30 Optional Calories

TIP: *Use vegetable based setting agent for the Chocolate Mousse when serving vegetarians.*

Chocolate Mousse

Ingredients:

1½ tablespoons cocoa
1 tablespoon cornflour
¾ pint (450ml) skimmed milk
few drops of vanilla essence
artificial sweetener
3 tablespoons hot water
¼ teaspoon coffee powder
1 sachet gelatine
2 large egg whites
pinch of cream of tartar
½oz (15g) white chocolate

Method:

1) Blend the cocoa and cornflour together with the milk. Add the vanilla essence and pour the cocoa mixture into a saucepan. Bring to the boil, stirring all the time. Boil for 1-2 minutes, sweeten to taste with artificial sweetener.

2) Pour the hot water into a cup, add the coffee powder and sprinkle in the gelatine, stand the cup in a saucepan of simmering water and leave until the gelatine has dissolved.

3) Stir the gelatine into the chocolate sauce and leave until cool and beginning to set.

4) Whisk the egg whites together with the cream of tartar then fold into the setting mixture. Spoon into four glasses and leave until set.

5) Grate the white chocolate over the top of each serving.

Selections per serving: ¼ Milk, 30 Optional Calories

Cheesy Dessert

Ingredients:

8oz (240g) cottage cheese with pineapple
2oz (60g) dried dates, stoned
5fl oz (150ml) low-fat natural yogurt
¼ pint (150ml) skimmed milk
2 teaspoons lemon juice
1 tablespoon frozen concentrated orange juice, thawed
artificial sweetener (optional)
2 tablespoons hot water
1 sachet gelatine

Method:

1) Place the cottage cheese with pineapple in the goblet of a liquidiser.

2) Roughly chop the dates and add to the cottage cheese together with the yogurt, milk, lemon juice and orange juice. Process to a purée.

3) Pour the purée into a bowl and add a little artificial sweetener if desired.

4) Pour the hot water into a small bowl or cup, sprinkle in the gelatine and stand in a saucepan of simmering water. Leave until the gelatine has completely dissolved.

5) Stir the dissolved gelatine into the cottage cheese, purée then pour the purée into four serving glasses and chill until set.

Selections per serving: ½ Fruit, ¼ Milk, 1 Protein, 30 Optional Calories

TIP: *Use vegetable based setting agent for the Cheesy Dessert when serving vegetarians.*

Stirred Rice Pudding☆

Ingredients:

2oz (60g) pudding rice
1 pint (600ml) skimmed milk
1 tablespoon sugar

Method:

1) Place the rice in a sieve and rinse under running cold water then place in a heavy-based saucepan.

2) Stir the milk together with the rice and bring to the boil over a low to moderate heat.

3) Reduce the heat as low as possible – the milk should be steaming rather than boiling. Cover the saucepan and leave to cook for 50-60 minutes stirring every 10 minutes.

4) When the rice is cooked remove the saucepan from the heat and stir in the sugar. Serve this pudding on its own or increase the number of portions and serve with fruit, but remember to adjust the Selections and Optional Calories as necessary.

Selections per serving: 1 Bread, 1 Milk, 30 Optional Calories

Crêpes Suzette ☆

Ingredients:

4oz (120g) plain flour
pinch of salt
grated zest of ½ lemon
1 egg
½ pint (300ml) skimmed milk
1 tablespoon oil
2 medium oranges
1 tablespoon caster sugar
3 tablespoons brandy

Method:

1) Make the crêpes as described in the pancake recipe (p.45).

2) Fold the pancakes into quarters.

3) Squeeze the juice from the oranges, pour into the frying pan, add the sugar and heat gently until the sugar has dissolved. Add the pancakes and heat gently. When thoroughly heated through warm the brandy, pour over and ignite, serve immediately.

Selections per serving: 1 Bread, ¾ Fat, ½ Fruit, ¼ Milk, ¼ Protein, 45 Optional Calories

TIP: *Pancakes freeze well – layer them with a film of plastic or greaseproof paper between, then thaw out when required.*

Lentil and Egg Savoury ☆

Ingredients:

2 teaspoons oil
1 onion, chopped
¼ teaspoon ground coriander
¼ teaspoon ground cumin
large pinch of hot chilli powder
½ teaspoon marjoram
4oz (120g) celeriac, chopped
4oz (120g) carrots, chopped
3oz (90g) split red lentils
8fl oz (240ml) stock
4 eggs
½ teaspoon salt
3oz (90g) hard cheese, grated

Method:

1) Heat the oil in a saucepan, add the onion and stir round, then cover the saucepan and leave over a low heat to cook very gently for 5 minutes.

2) Stir the spices and marjoram into the onion, stir well then add the vegetables, lentils and stock.

3) Bring the lentil and vegetable mixture to the boil, stirring all the time. Cover the saucepan, reduce the heat and leave to cook for 20 minutes or until the lentils and vegetables are cooked.

4) Place the eggs in a saucepan of cold water, add the salt and bring to the boil and boil for 10 minutes. Drain the eggs, remove the shells and cut each egg in half.

5) Transfer the lentil mixture to the goblet of a liquidiser and process to a purée.

6) Pour the lentil purée back into the saucepan and bring to the boil, stirring all the time. Sprinkle the grated cheese into the boiling lentil mixture, remove from the heat and stir until the cheese has melted.

7) Arrange two halves of egg on four serving plates then spoon over the hot lentil and cheese sauce.

Selections per serving: ¾ Bread, ½ Fat, 1¾ Protein, 1¼ Vegetable

Crêpes Suzette

Leek and Walnut Flan (See page 52) and Stuffed Figs (See page 57)

VEGETARIAN

Christmas Dinner

Menu

Melon

Nut Rissoles with Chilli Sauce

Nutty Brussels & Carrots

Christmas Pudding with Custard Sauce

Chewy Fruit Thins

Coffee

Melon ☆

Serves 6
30 Calories per serving

Ingredients:

3 medium Cantaloupe or Ogen melons
Ginger to taste

Method:

1) Cut the melons in half and scoop out the seeds. Using a teaspoon or melon baller, remove the melon from its skin.

2) Replace the melon balls in the four skin halves and sprinkle with ginger.

Selections per serving: 1 Fruit

Nut Rissoles with Chilli Sauce ☆

Serves 6
260 Calories per serving

Ingredients:

4oz (120g) bread
12oz (360g) tofu
2 onions
3oz (90g) roasted hazelnuts, finely chopped
3oz (90g) walnuts, finely chopped
½ teaspoon vegetable extract
2 eggs, beaten
2 small cans chopped tomatoes
2 teaspoons cornflour
½ teaspoon oregano
approximately 2 teaspoons chilli sauce
sprigs of oregano or coriander

Method:

1) Place the bread in a blender, process to form breadcrumbs, add the tofu and process once again until smooth. Transfer to a bowl.

2) Grate half the onion into the tofu mixture. Stir in the nuts and vegetable extract, blend well. Bind together with the egg.

3) Shape the tofu mixture into six rissoles, place on a baking tray and grill for 10-12 minutes until golden turning once.

4) Sieve the tomatoes, blend a little of the juice with the cornflour and put to one side.

5) Grate the remaining onion into the tomato juice, add the cornflour and bring to the boil. Boil for 1-2 minutes. Add oregano and chilli sauce to taste.

6) Serve the hot rissoles with the chilli sauce garnished with sprigs of oregano or coriander.

Selections per serving: ½ Bread, 1 Fat, 3 Protein, 1¼ Vegetable, 20 Optional Calories

Nutty Brussels ☆

Ingredients:

18 small chestnuts
1lb 4oz (600g) Brussels sprouts
salt
1 tablespoon olive oil
1 large red pepper, cored and cut into strips

Method:

1) Plunge the chestnuts into a saucepan of boiling water, simmer for 12 minutes then drain. Allow the nuts to cool a little then peel away the brown skins.

2) Remove the outer coarse skins from the Brussels sprouts, cut in half then place in a saucepan and cover with boiling water. Add a little salt and boil for 4-5 minutes until hot and partially cooked, they must remain crisp.

3) Heat the olive oil in a saucepan, add the red pepper and stir over a moderate heat for 1-2 minutes, add the drained Brussels sprouts and chestnuts and stir round for 1-2 minutes.

Selections per serving: ½ Bread, ½ Fat, 1 Vegetable

Carrots ☆

Ingredients:

1lb 2oz (540g) carrots, sliced

Method:

1) Place the sliced carrots in saucepan and cook in slightly salted water until cooked but firm.

2) Strain and place in a warm serving dish.

Chewy Fruit Thins ☆

Ingredients:

6oz (180g) raisins
¾oz (22g) Brazil nut kernels
3 teaspoons brandy
rice paper

Method:

1) Place the raisins, nuts and brandy in the goblet of a liquidiser. Process to a thick purée.

2) Spoon the fruit mixture onto a piece of rice paper.

3) Spread the fruit mixture out a little then lay a piece of rice paper over and, using a rolling pin, roll the mixture to form a rectangle about 4-5 inch (10-12.5cm) square. Refrigerate for 30-40 minutes or longer if time allows.

4) Using a sharp knife cut the rice paper square into sixteen small squares, arrange on a small plate and chill until required.

Selections per serving: 1 Fruit, ¼ Protein, 10 Optional Calories

Christmas Pudding – *(see page 13).*

Custard Sauce – *(see page 46).*

Total Selection per serving for complete meal:- 2 Bread, 1½ Fat, 3¼ Fruit, ¼ Milk, 3¼ Protein, 3 Vegetable, 160 Optional Calories

Simple Tofu ☆

Ingredients:

6oz (180g) tofu
2 teaspoons sesame oil
1 tablespoon soy sauce
1 teaspoon sesame seeds
2-3 spring onions, finely chopped

Method:

1) Cut the tofu into ½ inch (1.25cm) cubes.

2) Heat the sesame oil in a saucepan, add the tofu and stir-fry for 2-3 minutes until very hot.

3) Add the soy sauce and sesame seeds to the saucepan and stir over a low heat for about 40 seconds.

4) Spoon the tofu mixture onto a serving plate and sprinkle over the chopped spring onions.

Selections per serving: 2 Fat, 2 Protein,
20 Optional Calories

TIP: *Cover any remaining tofu with cold water and store in the refrigerator for use the next day.*

Leek and Walnut Flan ☆

Ingredients:

8 inch (20cm) cooked pastry flan case
12oz (360g) leeks
4 teaspoons margarine
4oz (120g) curd cheese
4 tablespoons skimmed milk
2 eggs
2oz (60g) walnut kernels

Method:

1) Place the flan case on a baking sheet and set aside.

2) Thinly slice the leeks.

3) Heat the margarine in a saucepan, add the leeks, stir round then cover the saucepan and leave over a very low heat for 10 minutes until the leeks are limp.

4) Reserve eight slices of leek then place the remainder in a liquidiser, add the curd cheese and milk and process to a purée.

5) Add the eggs to the liquidiser and process once again, just for a few seconds to mix all the ingredients together. Stir the purée into a bowl.

6) Finely chop the walnuts. Stir the walnuts into the leek purée.

7) Spoon the leek and walnut mixture into the cooked flan case, arrange the reserved slices of leek on the top and bake in a preheated oven at 350F, 180C, Gas Mark 4 for about 35 minutes or until firm to touch.

Selections per serving: ½ Bread, ¾ Fat, 1 Protein,
½ Vegetable,
50 Optional Calories

Vegetarian Shepherd's Pie ☆

Serves 4
225 Calories per serving

Ingredients:

1 tablespoon margarine
6oz (180g) leeks, thinly sliced
6oz (180g) mushrooms, roughly chopped
4oz (120g) beef flavoured soya protein
water or stock
6oz (180g) baked beans in tomato sauce
1 tablespoon tomato ketchup
1lb 2oz (540g) potatoes
salt
4 tablespoons skimmed milk
pepper

Method:

1) Heat the margarine in a saucepan, add the leeks and stir-fry over a low heat until the leeks are soft. Add the mushrooms, stir round then cover and leave for 3 minutes.

2) Weigh the soya then place in a measuring jug to measure its volume. Stir the soya into the mushroom mixture then measure double its volume of water or stock.

3) Pour the water or stock into the saucepan and stir well then add the baked beans in tomato sauce and tomato ketchup.

4) Bring the soya mixture to the boil, stirring all the time, reduce the heat as low as possible and leave to simmer for 5-6 minutes.

5) Cut the potatoes into chunks then cook in boiling salted water.

6) Spoon the soya mixture into a deep ovenproof dish.

7) Mash the potatoes with the milk and season to taste with salt and pepper. Pile the potatoes on top of the soya mixture then roughen the surface with a fork and brown under a hot grill.

Selections per serving: 1½ Bread, ¾ Fat, 2½ Protein, 1 Vegetable, 10 Optional Calories

TIP: *Many meat eaters will enjoy the Vegetarian Shepherd's Pie – don't restrict it to vegetarians.*

Prune Smoothie ☆

Serves 2
125 Calories per serving

Ingredients:

4oz (120g) ready-to-eat prunes
2 inch (5cm) strip of lemon zest
4fl oz (120ml) water
4oz (120g) tofu
¼ pint (150ml) skimmed milk
lemon juice

Method:

1) Place the prunes and lemon zest in a saucepan, add the water, cover and simmer for 12-15 minutes until cooked.

2) Leave the prunes to cool then remove their stones and the strip of lemon zest.

3) Place the prunes, together with the tofu and milk, into the goblet of a liquidiser. Liquidise to a purée.

4) Add a generous amount of lemon juice to suit your taste. Chill until ready to serve.

Selections per serving: 2 Fruit, ¼ Milk, ½ Protein, 10 Optional Calories

Vegetarian Goulash ☆

Ingredients:

6oz (180g) onions
1 large green pepper
2 teaspoons oil
1½ tablespoons paprika
2oz (60g) split red lentils
8oz (227g) can tomatoes
4fl oz (120ml) stock
9oz (270g) tofu

Method:

1) Thinly slice the onions then separate into rings. Remove the seeds from the green pepper then thinly slice.

2) Heat the oil in a saucepan, add the onions and green pepper and stir round, then cover the saucepan and leave over a low heat for 10-12 minutes.

3) Stir the paprika into the onion and pepper. Add the lentils, tomatoes and stock. Break the tomatoes up with a wooden spoon.

4) Cut the tofu into 1 inch (2.5cm) cubes, add to the saucepan then cover and leave to simmer for about 20 minutes, stirring occasionally, until the lentils are cooked.

Selections per serving: 1 Fat, 2½ Protein, 3 Vegetable

TIP: *Serve the Spinach and Lentil Soup with warm crusty wholemeal rolls.*

Spinach and Lentil Soup ☆

Ingredients:

1 small onion
6oz (180g) spinach
2 teaspoons margarine
3oz (90g) split red lentils
½ pint (300ml) vegetable stock
garlic purée
whole nutmeg
¼ pint (150ml) skimmed milk
salt and pepper

Method:

1) Chop the onion. Wash the spinach in two or three changes of water.

2) Melt the margarine in a saucepan, add the onion, and stir-fry for 4-5 minutes or until soft.

3) Shake as much of the moisture as possible from the spinach leaves. Tear any large leaves into three or four pieces then add all the leaves to the saucepan. Cover and cook over a low heat for 6 minutes until the spinach is limp.

4) Stir the lentils into the saucepan together with the stock, a little garlic purée – just enough to cover the tip of a knife, and a generous grating of nutmeg.

5) Cover the saucepan and cook for 12 minutes or until the lentils are cooked.

6) Transfer the spinach and lentil mixture to a liquidiser and process to a purée.

7) Pour the purée into a saucepan, stir in the milk and season with salt and pepper. Stir over a moderate heat until boiling then ladle into soup bowls and grate fresh nutmeg over.

Selections per serving: 1 Fat, ¼ Milk, 1½ Protein, 1½ Vegetable

Lentil Pie ☆

Serves 4
285 Calories per serving

Ingredients:

2 onions
4oz (120g) carrots
3oz (90g) celery
4 teaspoons margarine
8fl oz (240ml) tomato and vegetable juice
8fl oz (240ml) water
5oz (150g) split lentils
1lb (480g) parsnips
salt
3 tablespoons skimmed milk
1½ oz (45g) hard cheese, finely grated

Method:

1) Thinly slice the onions. Dice the carrots and celery.

2) Heat 2 teaspoons margarine in a saucepan, add the onions and stir-fry for 1-2 minutes. Cover the saucepan and reduce the heat as low as possible and leave to cook for 4 minutes or until the onions are soft and just cooked.

3) Stir the tomato and vegetable juice, water, lentils, carrots and celery into the saucepan then cover and simmer gently for 20 minutes, stirring occasionally.

4) While the lentils are simmering, cut the parsnips into chunks and cook in boiling salted water then drain and mash with the milk.

5) Remove the cooked lentils from the heat, add the cheese and stir until melted.

6) Spoon the lentil mixture into a flameproof dish, spread the mashed parsnips over and dot with the remaining margarine. Brown under a hot grill.

Selections per serving: 1 Bread, 1 Fat, ¼ Fruit,
1½ Protein, 1 Vegetable,
10 Optional Calories

TIP: *To make an appetising snack, serve the Savoury Pittas with a colourful mixed salad.*

Savoury Pittas ☆

Serves 2
205 Calories per serving

Ingredients:

2 × 1oz (30g) pittas
2oz (60g) curd cheese
2oz (60g) cottage cheese
3 large black olives, stoned
½oz (15g) Parmesan cheese, finely grated
½oz (15g) walnuts
salt and pepper

Method:

1) Make a 3 inch (7.5cm) slit along the edge of each pitta.

2) Mash the curd and cottage cheeses together.

3) Finely chop the black olives and mix into the cheese mixture, add the Parmesan cheese.

4) Roughly chop the walnuts and add to the cheese mixture, then season well with salt and pepper.

5) Spread the cheese mixture evenly into each pitta then cook under a hot grill for 2-3 minutes, turning once, until the bread is crisp and the filling warm.

Selections per serving: 1 Bread, ½ Fat, 1¾ Protein

Nutty Spaghetti ☆

Serves 2
395 Calories per serving

Ingredients:

4oz (120g) spaghetti
salt
2 tablespoons peanut butter
3 tablespoons skimmed milk
1oz (30g) roasted peanuts

Method:

1) Cook the spaghetti in boiling salted water according to the packaging instructions.

2) Place the peanut butter in a bowl, gradually blend in the milk.

3) Chop the peanuts and add to the blended mixture.

4) Drain the hot spaghetti, mix the peanut mixture thoroughly through the spaghetti and serve.

Selections per serving: 2 Bread, 1½ Fat, 2 Protein, 10 Optional Calories

TIP: *Take care when baking mushrooms, the moisture oozes out if they are overcooked.*

Stuffed Mushrooms ☆

Serves 4
135 Calories per serving

Ingredients:

2oz (60g) long grain rice
salt
1 tablespoon margarine
4 large cap mushrooms – each approx
*   1½-2oz (45-60g)*
1 onion, finely chopped
½oz (15g) mixture of nuts, chopped
1oz (30g) Parmesan cheese, finely grated
scant ¼ teaspoon mixed herbs

Method:

1) Cook the rice in boiling salted water according to the packaging instructions.

2) Lightly grease an ovenproof dish just large enough to hold all the mushrooms with a little of the margarine.

3) Remove the mushroom stalks, reserve the caps and finely chop the stalks.

4) Melt the remaining margarine in a saucepan, add the onion and stir-fry for 4-5 minutes until cooked and beginning to brown, add the chopped mushrooms and continue cooking for 2-3 minutes.

5) Mix the onion mixture together with the nuts, drained rice, half to three quarters of the cheese and the mixed herbs.

6) Place the mushrooms, dark side uppermost in the greased dish and pile the rice stuffing on top of each one. Sprinkle the remaining cheese over and bake at 375F, 190C, Gas Mark 5 for 12 minutes or until the mushrooms are cooked. Brown under a preheated grill.

Selections per serving: ½ Bread, ¾ Fat, ½ Protein, ¾ Vegetable, 5 Optional Calories

Crispy Vegetables☆

Ingredients:

½ onion
4oz (120g) carrots
4oz (120g) swede
4oz (120g) cabbage, Savoy if possible
1 tablespoon sesame oil
1 tablespoon soy sauce
½oz (15g) pistachio kernels

Method:

1) Chop the onion.

2) Cut the carrots and swede into 1½ inch (4cm) lengths no more than ¼ inch (5mm) wide.

3) Shred the cabbage.

4) Heat the oil in a wok or frying pan, add the onion and stir-fry for 3 minutes.

5) Add the carrots and swede to the pan and stir-fry for 4-5 minutes until hot and half cooked. Add the cabbage and continue stir-frying for a further 2-3 minutes until the cabbage is bright green and cooked but still crisp.

6) Sprinkle the soy sauce and pistachio nuts over the vegetables, stir well then serve.

Selections per serving: 1½ Fat, ½ Protein, 2¼ Vegetable, 10 Optional Calories

TIP: *Prepare figs just before serving so they remain moist and colourful.*

Stuffed Figs☆

Ingredients:

4 fresh figs
½ medium banana
½ teaspoon lemon juice
2oz (60g) curd cheese
1 tablespoon soured cream
¼oz (10g) toasted hazelnut kernels, chopped
1 kiwi fruit, sliced as thinly as possible

Method:

1) Cut the figs into four quarters, leaving them attached at the base so the fig quarters separate like petals of a flower.

2) Mash the banana together with the lemon juice. Gradually mix in the curd cheese and cream.

3) Reserve a few nuts, add the remainder to the cheese mixture.

4) Spoon a quarter of the cheese mixture into the centre of each fig.

5) Slice the kiwi fruit into very thin slices, then arrange round each fig.

6) Sprinkle the reserved hazelnuts over the cheese filling then serve.

Selections per serving: 1 Fruit, ¼ Protein, 25 Optional Calories

Cauliflower with Peanut Sauce ☆

Ingredients:

1 medium cauliflower
1oz (30g) cornflour
½ pint (300ml) skimmed milk
4 tablespoons peanut butter
salt and pepper
¾oz (20g) dry roasted peanuts, roughly chopped

Method:

1) Trim the cauliflower and leave whole or cut in quarters then boil or steam until cooked but still a little crisp.

2) Blend the cornflour with a little milk to form a smooth paste, stir in the remaining milk and bring to the boil stirring all the time.

3) Spoon the peanut butter into a jug, gradually blend in the white sauce then pour back into the saucepan and bring to the boil, stirring all the time. Season to taste with salt and pepper.

4) Drain the cauliflower and place in a warm bowl. Pour the hot peanut sauce over and sprinkle with the chopped peanuts.

Selections per serving: ¼ Bread, 1 Fat, ¼ Milk, 1¼ Protein, 1½ Vegetable, 15 Optional Calories

TIP: *When using peanut butter in recipes, add salt cautiously as the butter already contains a high proportion of salt.*

Tofu Batter Pudding ☆

Ingredients:

4oz (120g) plain white flour – preferably strong bread flour
salt
1 large egg – size 1 or 2
½ pint (300ml) skimmed milk
1 tablespoon oil
6oz (180g) smoked tofu

Method:

1) Sieve the flour and a pinch of salt into a bowl, make a well in the centre and break the egg into it.

2) Add a little milk to the egg then gradually beat the egg and milk together drawing the flour into the mixture. Continue until all the milk is mixed into the batter. Set aside for 15-20 minutes.

3) Place the oil in a 7½-8 inch (17.5-20cm) square baking tin.

4) Cut the smoked tofu into small dice and add to the oil. Place the tin in a hot oven 425-450F, 210-220C, Gas Mark 7-8. Leave the tin in the oven for 8-10 minutes until the oil is bubbling and the tofu very hot.

5) Stir the batter and pour into the hot tin. Bake for 35-40 minutes until it has risen high and turned crisp and golden brown. Serve immediately.

Selections per serving: 1 Bread, ¾ Fat, ¼ Milk, 1 Protein

Creamy Bean Mix ☆

Serves 4
135 Calories per serving

Ingredients:

1 teaspoon margarine
1 tablespoon grated onion
15oz (450g) drained canned flageolet beans
6 tablespoons single cream
salt and pepper
nutmeg

Method:

1) Melt the margarine in a saucepan, add the onion and stir over a moderate heat for 2 minutes.

2) Stir the beans and cream into the saucepan and bring slowly to the boil, stirring all the time.

3) Season the Creamy Bean Mix generously with salt, pepper and freshly grated nutmeg.

Selections per serving: ¼ Fat, 1¼ Protein
75 Optional Calories

☙☙☙☙☙☙☙☙☙☙☙☙☙☙☙☙☙☙☙☙☙☙☙☙☙☙☙☙☙☙☙☙☙☙

TIP: *Serve the Blue Cheese Dressing with a variety of savoury salads. It adds a great deal of flavour.*

☙☙☙☙☙☙☙☙☙☙☙☙☙☙☙☙☙☙☙☙☙☙☙☙☙☙☙☙☙☙☙☙☙☙

Blue Cheese Salad ☆

Serves 2
160 Calories per serving

Ingredients:

a few sprigs of Lamb's lettuce
½ red or yellow pepper, cored and cut in half rings
1 stick celery, chopped
1 tablespoon spring onions, chopped
4 endive leaves
1 medium seedless orange

For the dressing:

2oz (60g) blue cheese such as Gorgonzola or Danish blue
1 teaspoon olive oil
2-3 tablespoons cider or white wine vinegar
salt and pepper

Method:

1) Place the Lamb's lettuce, red or yellow pepper, celery and spring onions in a salad bowl.

2) Tear the endive leaves into pieces and add to the salad.

3) Using a sharp knife, cut the peel and pith off the orange, cut in half lengthways, then slice. Mix into the salad.

4) Make the dressing. Grate or crumble the cheese into a small bowl, mash with a fork and gradually add the oil and vinegar. Season to taste.

5) Serve the salad and dressing separately. Spoon the dressing over the salad just before eating.

Selections per serving: ½ Fat, ½ Fruit, 1 Protein,
1¼ Vegetable

Savoury Macaroni ☆

Ingredients:

4oz (120g) macaroni
salt
½ large red pepper
½ medium onion
2oz (60g) mushrooms
2 teaspoons margarine
1oz (30g) flour
¾ pint (450ml) skimmed milk
6oz (180g) smoked tofu
4oz (120g) hard cheese, grated

Method:

1) Cook the macaroni in boiling salted water according to the packaging instructions.

2) Remove the seeds from the red pepper and chop. Chop the onion and mushrooms.

3) Heat the margarine in a saucepan, add the red pepper and onion and stir round, then cover and leave over a low heat for 5 minutes.

4) Add the mushrooms to the saucepan, cover and leave for 2 minutes.

5) Stir the flour into the vegetable mixture, stir round then remove from the heat and gradually blend in the milk. Bring to the boil stirring all the time.

6) Cut the tofu into ¾ inch (2cm) cubes, add to the vegetable mixture. Mix in the macaroni then add about three-quarters of the cheese, stir well until the cheese has melted.

7) Spoon the macaroni and vegetables into a flameproof dish, sprinkle over the reserved cheese and brown under a hot grill.

Selections per serving: 1¼ Bread, ½ Fat, ¼ Milk, 1¾ Protein, ½ Vegetable, 10 Optional Calories

---

TIP: *Substitute the macaroni with multi-coloured pasta shapes to make a colourful alternative.*

Sesame Savoy *(for Vegetarians only)*

Ingredients:

½ small onion
7-8oz (210-240g) Savoy cabbage
salt
1 teaspoon sesame oil
1 tablespoon tahini
2 teaspoons sesame seeds

Method:

1) Finely chop the onion.

2) Wash the cabbage and lay the leaves on top of each other. Cut across the cabbage in 1-inch (2.5cm) slices.

3) Cook the cabbage in boiling salted water or steam until hot but still crisp.

4) Heat the oil in a saucepan, add the onion and stir-fry for 3-4 minutes until cooked.

5) Add the tahini to the saucepan, stir well then add the drained cabbage. Stir continuously over a moderate heat for 30 seconds, just long enough to coat all the cabbage.

6) Spoon the cabbage into a warm bowl, sprinkle with the sesame seeds and serve.

Selections per serving: ½ Fat, ¾ Vegetable, 25 Optional Calories

Savoury Macaroni

Beef Stew (See page 64) and Fish Risotto (See page 65)

MEAT, POULTRY, FISH

Christmas Dinner

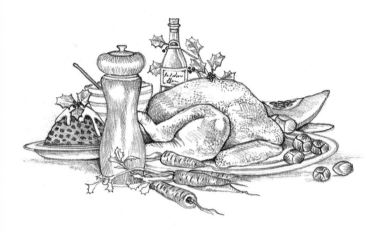

Menu

Melon

*Roast Turkey, Stuffing,
Bread Sauce*

Brussels Sprouts, Carrots

Cranberry & Port Sauce

*Christmas Pudding with
Custard Sauce*

Coffee

Melon

**Serves 8
30 Calories per serving**

Ingredients:

*4 medium Cantaloupe or Ogen melons
Ginger to taste*

Method:

1) Cut the melons in half and scoop out the seeds. Using a teaspoon or melon baller, remove the melon from its skin.

2) Replace the melon balls in the four skin halves and sprinkle with ginger.

Selections per serving: 1 Fruit

Stuffing

**Serves 16 portions
70 Calories per serving**

Ingredients:

*3 x ½oz (15g) lean rashers back bacon, derinded
3 tablespoons margarine
2 onions, finely chopped
8oz (240g) mushrooms, finely chopped
2 tablespoons parsley
8oz (240g) dry bread
1 tablespoon lemon juice
1 large egg, lightly beaten*

Method:

1) Lay the bacon on the rack of a grill pan and cook, under a moderate grill, turning once, until cooked but not crisp. Allow to cool and chop finely.

2) Heat the margarine in a saucepan, add the onions and stir-fry for 5-6 minutes. Add the mushrooms to the saucepan and continue frying for about 4 minutes until cooked. Stir in the parsley and set aside.

3) Break the bread into pieces, place in a liquidiser or food processor and process to breadcrumbs.

4) Stir the breadcrumbs into the onion and mushroom mixture, mix in the lemon juice and bind together with the egg.

Selections per serving: Stuffing alone – ½ Bread, ½ Fat, ¼ Protein, 50 Optional Calories

Turkey

120 Calories per serving

Ingredients:

11½-12½ lb (5.5-6kg) fresh turkey with giblets
1 large onion
2½ tablespoons margarine

Method:

1) Remove the giblets from the turkey. Rinse the bird under cold running water and pat dry with kitchen paper.

2) Spoon the stuffing into the skin at neck of bird. Place the onion in the body of the turkey.

3) Spread the margarine thickly over the breast of the turkey then spread over the rest of the bird.

4) Cover with foil and cook at 400-425 F, 200-210 C, Gas Mark 6-7 for 3 hours, 15 minutes. Remove the foil, baste well with the juices from the roasting tin and continue cooking, uncovered, for about 30 minutes until brown and completely cooked.

5) Transfer to a warm serving plate and leave to stand while preparing the gravy.

6) Carve the turkey, allowing 3oz (90g) meat per person. Serve the hot turkey with all the gravy and half the stuffing for eight people on Christmas Day, then the same quantity of meat and stuffing cold, at a later date.

Selections per serving: 3 Protein (without stuffing)

Gravy

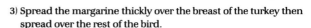

Serves 8
5 Calories per serving

Ingredients:

Giblets from turkey
1 onion, sliced
1 tablespoon cornflour
1 pint (600ml) water

Method:

1) Remove giblets from the turkey, rinse under cold running water and pat dry with kitchen paper.

2) Place giblets in an ovenproof dish with sliced onion and add about 1 pint (600ml) water to cover.

3) Cover the dish and place on lowest shelf of the oven. When the turkey is cooked remove from the oven and leave to stand for about 10 minutes.

4) Place the giblets and juices from the turkey roasting pan into a basin standing in a bowl of chilled water – if possible add a few ice cubes to the chilled water. As soon as the fat solidifies on the top, skim it off. Blend the cornflour with a little cold water to form a smooth paste.

5) Strain the giblets and gradually stir the juices into the cornflour. Pour into a saucepan and bring to the boil, stirring all the time. Boil for 2 minutes then pour into a gravy boat or jug.

Selections per serving: 5 Optional Calories

Brussels Sprouts and Carrots

Serves 8
30 Calories per serving

Ingredients:

1lb 8oz (720g) Brussels sprouts
1lb 8oz (720g) carrots, sliced
salt

Method:

1) Remove any coarse outer leaves from the Brussels sprouts then cut a cross through the base of each one.

2) Place the Brussels sprouts and carrots in separate saucepans and cook in slightly salted water.

3) Strain the vegetables and place in a warm serving dish.

Selections per serving: 2 Vegetable

Bread Sauce

Serves 8
45 Calories per serving

Ingredients:

1 onion
4 whole cloves
few peppercorns
blade of mace (optional)
12fl oz (360ml) skimmed milk
2½oz (75g) fresh breadcrumbs
1 tablespoon double cream
salt

Method:

1) Peel the onion and press the cloves into it. Place the onion, peppercorns and mace in a small saucepan. Pour in the milk and heat very gently until the milk is steaming and just reaching boiling point. Remove from the heat and leave for 30 minutes.

2) Remove the peppercorns, mace and onion. Stir in the breadcrumbs and cream and return to a very low heat. Bring to the boil, stirring all the time. Remove from the heat, season with salt and serve.

Selections per serving: ¼ Bread, 25 Optional Calories

Cranberry & Port Sauce

Serves 8
25 Calories per serving

Ingredients:

8oz (240g) cranberries
¼ pt (150ml) water
1 teaspoon arrowroot or cornflour
2 tablespoons sugar
3 tablespoons port

Method:

1) Place the cranberries and water in a small saucepan over a moderate heat. Simmer for 10-15 minutes until cranberries are cooked. Stir briskly to break up some of the cranberries to make a purée containing a few whole cranberries.

2) Blend the arrowroot or cornflour to a smooth paste with 2-3 teaspoons cold water. Stir into the cranberries and bring to the boil, stirring all the time. Boil for 2 minutes.

3) Remove the sauce from the heat and stir in the sugar and port. Serve hot or leave until cool.

Selections per serving: ¼ Fruit, 25 Optional Calories

Christmas Pudding – *(see page 13)*.

Custard Sauce – *(see page 46)*.

Total Selection per serving for complete meal:- 1¾ Bread, ½ Fat, 2¾ Fruit, ½ Milk, 3½ Protein, 2¼ Vegetable, 115 Optional Calories

Beef Stew and Dumplings

Serves 4
395 Calories per serving

Ingredients:

14oz (420g) stewing beef
14fl oz (420ml) stock
2 teaspoons cornflour
2 sticks celery, 4oz (120g) leeks
8oz (240g) parsnips
14oz (420g) mixture of kohlrabi, swede, carrot, Jerusalem artichoke, turnip
2 teaspoons vinegar
1 bay leaf, salt and pepper
3½oz (105g) self-raising flour
¼ teaspoon baking powder
½ teaspoon mixed herbs
2½ tablespoons margarine

Method:

1) Place the beef in a saucepan or flameproof casserole, cover with the 420ml stock and bring to the boil over a low heat. Simmer gently for 3-4 minutes then cool rapidly and skim off all the fat that rises to the surface of the stock.

2) Cut the beef into 1½ inch (4cm) cubes and place in a casserole dish. Sprinkle the cornflour and stir well.

3) Slice the celery and leeks into 1½-2 inch (4-5cm) lengths. Cut the parsnips and other vegetables into large cubes and add all the vegetables to the meat. Stir in the stock, add the vinegar, bay leaf and a little salt and pepper.

4) Cook at 325F, 160C, Gas Mark 3 for 2 hours, stirring once or twice during the cooking time.

5) Sieve the flour and baking powder into a bowl, add the herbs and rub in the margarine, if possible margarine which has been stored in the freezer, into the flour.

6) Mix cold water into the flour mixture to form a soft dough. Divide into eight pieces and shape into balls. Add the dumplings to the casserole, cover and continue cooking at the same temperature for about 20 minutes or until the dumplings are cooked.

Selections per serving: 1¼ Bread, 1¾ Fat, 3 Protein, 1¾ Vegetable, 20 Optional Calories

Fish Risotto

Ingredients:

few grains of saffron
4 tablespoons warm water
6oz (180g) live mussels
10oz (300g) boneless monkfish
2 tablespoons oil
1 onion, chopped
8oz (240g) long grain rice
4oz (120g) leeks, sliced
1 red pepper, chopped
2oz (60g) mushrooms, sliced
2½oz (75g) peeled prawns
2 tablespoons chopped coriander

Method:

1) Place the saffron in a bowl, add the warm water and leave for 2-3 hours, or longer, to allow the flavour and colour to develop.

2) Wash the mussels well under running cold water, pull off any weed hanging from the shells, then wash again. Discard any mussels which remain open or which feel heavy.

3) Cut the monkfish into ¾ inch (2cm) squares.

4) Heat 1 tablespoon oil in a saucepan, add the onion and stir round. Cover the saucepan and leave for 3-4 minutes. Stir the rice into the saucepan, stir well. Make the infused saffron water up to 14fl oz (420ml) – about 4fl oz (120ml) less than the recommended amount. Stir the water into the rice, cover and leave to cook over a low heat.

5) Heat 2 teaspoons oil in a separate saucepan, add the leeks and red pepper and stir round. Cover and leave over a low heat for 3 minutes. Add the remaining oil, mushrooms, monkfish and mussels. Cover the saucepan and cook for 2-3 minutes, shaking the pan occasionally. Cook until the mussels have opened wide, discard any that remain closed.

6) Five minutes before the end of the recommended cooking time for the rice add the mussel mixture, prawns and coriander. Stir well and leave over a low heat for the remaining cooking time, add a little more boiling water if necessary.

Selections per serving: 2 Bread, 1½ Fat, 3¼ Protein, 1¼ Vegetable

TIP: *To store live mussels overnight, place in a bowl of cold water and add a spoonful of porridge oats.*

Plaice and Celery

Ingredients:

2oz (60g) celery
½ tablespoon margarine
3 tablespoons weak stock
1 teaspoon chopped coriander
2 teaspoons cornflour
6 tablespoons skimmed milk
4oz (120g) skinned plaice fillet
salt and pepper

Method:

1) Chop the celery as finely as possible.

2) Melt the margarine in a saucepan, add the celery and stir round then add the stock and coriander.

3) Cover the saucepan and leave over a low heat for 15 minutes or until the celery is completely cooked.

4) Blend the cornflour with a little milk to form a smooth paste. Add the cornflour paste and the remaining milk to the saucepan and bring to the boil, stirring all the time. Boil for 2 minutes.

5) Cut the plaice into 1 inch (2.5cm) strips.

6) Stir the plaice into the boiling sauce, reduce the heat and simmer for about 3 minutes until the fish is cooked. Season with salt and pepper.

Selections per serving: 1½ Fat, 3 Protein, ¾ Vegetable, 50 Optional Calories

Devillish Herrings

Ingredients:

2 × 4oz (120g) herring fillets
6 capers, finely chopped
1 teaspoon Dijon mustard
½ teaspoon horseradish sauce
1 teaspoon tomato purée
½ teaspoon margarine

Method:

1) Lay the fillets, skin side down, on a working surface.

2) Mix the capers together with the mustard, horseradish and tomato purée. Spread the mixture evenly over the fillets then roll them up and secure in place with cocktail sticks or skewers.

3) Lightly grease a piece of foil with the margarine, lay the herrings on the foil then draw the foil up and fold loosely over the fish. Bake at 375F, 190C, Gas Mark 5 for 14-15 minutes.

Selections per serving: ¼ Fat, 3 Protein, 5 Optional Calories

TIP: *Buy fresh, dark green spinach leaves, don't purchase any which are beginning to turn yellow.*

Chicken Rolls

Ingredients:

4 × 3½ oz (105g) boned skinless chicken breasts
4 teaspoons margarine
½ medium onion, finely chopped
2oz (60g) spinach leaves – stalks removed
2oz (60g) fresh breadcrumbs
2 × ½oz (15g) rashers lean back bacon, derinded
1 medium orange, finely grated zest and juice
salt and pepper

Method:

1) Grease four squares of foil large enough to hold the chicken with 1-2 teaspoons margarine. Place the remaining margarine in a saucepan.

2) Melt the margarine over a moderate heat, add the onion and stir-fry for 4-5 minutes until soft.

3) Wash the spinach in several changes of water to remove all the grit on the leaves. Shake excess water from the leaves and dab dry with a piece of kitchen paper.

4) Roughly chop the spinach leaves then add to the onion. Stir over a low heat until the spinach softens and the leaves collapse. Remove from the heat and stir in the breadcrumbs.

5) Cook the bacon on a rack under a preheated grill then chop into small pieces and mix into the breadcrumb mixture. Stir in the orange zest and juice, season with salt and pepper.

6) Lay one chicken breast between two sheets of damp greaseproof paper then, using a steak hammer or rolling pin, beat the breast until two to two and half times its original size. Repeat with the other pieces of chicken.

7) Spoon a quarter of the spinach and orange stuffing over the chicken leaving a ½ inch (1.25cm) clear each side. Roll the chicken breast up and secure with a cocktail stick. Repeat with the remaining chicken.

8) Lay each chicken roll on a piece of greased foil then fold over to form a parcel. Place all the rolls slightly apart on a baking sheet, and cook at 375F, 190C, Gas Mark 5 for about 30 minutes until cooked.

Selections per serving: ½ Bread, 1 Fat, ¼ Fruit, 3 Protein, ¼ Vegetable

Curried Chicken Soup

Ingredients:

4oz (120g) Brussels sprouts
4oz (120g) skinned boneless chicken thighs or breasts
1 tablespoon oil
1½ tablespoons curry powder
1½ tablespoons flour
1½ pints (900ml) chicken stock
3 tablespoons tomato purée
6oz (180g) mixture of carrot and swede
1 large leek
5fl oz (150ml) low-fat natural yogurt

Method:

1) Halve or quarter the Brussels sprouts depending on their size. Cut the chicken into very small dice.

2) Heat the oil in a saucepan, add the chicken and stir over a moderate heat for 2-3 minutes until it has lost its pinkness.

3) Stir in the curry powder and flour then gradually blend in the stock. Add the tomato purée and all the vegetables.

4) Bring to the boil, cover and simmer for 25-30 minutes. Allow to cool for 3-4 minutes then stir in the yogurt and ladle into four warm soup bowls.

Selections per serving: ¾ Fat, ¼ Milk, ¾ Protein, 1¼ Vegetable, 20 Optional Calories

TIP: *Serve the cold Braised Pork with an unusual vegetable purée.*

Braised Pork

Ingredients:

3½lb (1.6kg) loin of pork
4 teaspoons oil
1 clove garlic, peeled but whole
10 shallots, halved
6 sticks celery, cut in ½ inch (1.25cm) slices
5 juniper berries, crushed
¾ teaspoon sage
8fl oz (240ml) apple juice
4fl oz (120ml) water
2 medium dessert apples, peeled, quartered and cored
salt and pepper

Method:

1) Ask your butcher to bone and remove all the fat and skin from the pork then roll it into a neat joint. A 3½lb (1.6kg) loin of pork should weigh about 2lbs (1.2 kg) when prepared.

2) Lay the joint on the rack of a grill pan and cook under a moderate heat, turning once, until the fat stops dripping – as there is very little fat this won't take long and the meat will brown a little.

3) Heat the oil in a large flameproof casserole dish. Add the garlic and stir-fry for 2 minutes then remove the garlic clove and add the shallots. Stir-fry the shallots for 4-5 minutes until beginning to brown. Add the celery, juniper berries, sage, apple juice and water and bring to the boil.

4) Lay the pork on top of the vegetables, add the apple quarters and season well with salt and pepper. Cover and cook at 300-325F, 150-160C, Gas Mark 2-3 for 2 hours 30 minutes or until the pork is cooked.

5) Lift the joint onto a plate and cut 3oz (90g) portions per serving, divide all the shallot and apple mixture between the eight portions. Reserve the remaining meat to serve cold.

Selections per serving: ½ Fat, ½ Fruit, 3 Protein, ½ Vegetable

Corned Beef Pie

Ingredients:

1 medium aubergine
salt
2 teaspoons margarine
1 small onion, chopped
2 teaspoons flour
14oz (400g) can chopped tomatoes
½ teaspoon celery seed
½ teaspoon oregano
10oz (300g) corned beef, cut into ¾ inch (2cm)
  cubes
1lb 2oz (520g) potatoes
4 tablespoons skimmed milk
1oz (30g) hard cheese, grated

Method:

1) Cut the auberine into 1-1½ inch (2.5-4cm) chunks, place in a sieve or colander and sprinkle liberally with salt. Leave for about 30 minutes to allow the bitter juices to drip away, then rinse well under running cold water.

2) Heat the margarine in a saucepan, add the onion and stir-fry for 5 minutes until beginning to brown, do not allow them to burn.

3) Remove the saucepan from the heat and stir in the flour. Stir in the chopped tomatoes, celery seed, oregano and aubergine. Cover the saucepan, bring to the boil then reduce the heat and leave to simmer for 10 minutes, stirring once or twice during the cooking time, add the corned beef and simmer for 4 minutes.

4) While the vegetable mixture is cooking cut the potatoes into chunks and cook in boiling salted water, then drain and mash with the milk.

5) Spoon the corned beef mixture into a flameproof dish, spoon the mashed potato over and sprinkle with the grated cheese. Place under a preheated grill and cook until golden brown.

Selections per serving: 1½ Bread, ½ Fat, 2¾ Protein,
                            3 Vegetable, 10 Optional Calories

---

TIP: *Stewing lamb is often cheap and ideal for casseroling but it contains a high proportion of fat so make sure you remove as much as possible.*

Lamb Casserole

Ingredients:

14oz (420g) lamb
6oz (180g) swede, cut into ½ inch (1.25cm) cubes
1 onion, roughly chopped
3oz (90g) drained canned sweetcorn
¾ teaspoon rosemary
1oz (30g) pearl barley
12fl oz (360ml) stock
salt and pepper

Method:

1) Place the lamb in a saucepan, pour over sufficient water to just cover, then gradually bring to the boil. Simmer gently for 5 minutes. Cool rapidly then skim off the fat which rises to the surface. Cut the meat into 1-1½ inch (2.5-4cm) cubes, place in an ovenproof casserole dish.

2) Add the swede, onion, sweetcorn, rosemary and pearl barley to the lamb. Stir in the stock and season with a little salt and pepper.

3) Cover the casserole and cook at 300-325F, 150-160C, Gas Mark 2-3, for 1 hour 30 minutes.

Selections per serving: ½ Bread, 3 Protein, 1 Vegetable

Turkey in Celery Sauce

Ingredients:

2 tablespoons margarine
1 medium onion, finely chopped
6fl oz (180ml) white wine
6oz (180g) celery, finely chopped
3oz (90g) seedless white grapes
12oz (360g) skinned boneless turkey or chicken
chicken stock if necessary

Method:

1) Place ½ tablespoon margarine in a saucepan, add the onion and stir-fry for 4 minutes.

2) Stir the wine and celery into the saucepan and bring to the boil, stir well then cover and leave to simmer for 20 minutes.

3) Place the grapes in a bowl, cover with boiling water and leave to stand for 1-2 minutes then drain and peel off the skins. Cut each grape in half.

4) Cut the turkey or chicken into ½ × 2½ inch (1.25 × 6.25cm) strips.

5) Heat half the remaining margarine in a saucepan, add about half the turkey or chicken and stir round for 1-2 minutes until the meat has lost its pink colour. Remove the meat with a slotted spoon and add the remaining margarine and cook the remaining turkey or chicken in the same way.

6) Pour the celery and wine mixture into a liquidiser and process to a purée. Pour the purée into a saucepan and add the meat. Bring the sauce to the boil, stir well then add the grapes and cover. Leave over a low heat for 8-10 minutes stirring occasionally or until the meat is cooked. If the sauce becomes very thick add a little chicken stock.

Selections per serving: 1½ Fat, ¼ Fruit, 2½ Protein, ¼ Vegetable, 40 Optional Calories

---

TIP: *Serve the Turkey in Celery Sauce with a selection of brightly coloured vegetables.*

Marinated Lamb

Ingredients:

2 racks of lamb each with six chops and all the surrounded skin and fat removed – prepared weight about 1lb 12oz (840g)
5fl oz (150ml) low-fat natural yogurt
1 large clove garlic, crushed
¼ inch (5mm) slice ginger
1 tablespoon grated onion
1 tablespoon lemon juice
1 teaspoon basil
1 teaspoon mint

Method:

1) Trim any small pieces of fat remaining between the chops.

2) Place the yogurt in a bowl, add the garlic, then peel and halve or quarter the ginger and press through the garlic press into the yogurt mixture.

3) Stir the onion, lemon juice, basil and mint into the yogurt and mix well.

4) Spoon the yogurt marinade over each rack of lamb then place the lamb in a suitable container and chill in the refrigerator for 12-24 hours.

5) Lay the racks of lamb on a rack resting in a baking tray, cover loosely with foil and cook at 375F, 190C, Gas Mark 5 for about 1 hour 10 minutes until cooked but just a little pink in the centre – if you prefer meat well-done return to the oven and continue cooking for 10-15 minutes.

Selections per serving: ¼ Milk, 3 Protein

Blue Cheese Beef

Serves 4
295 Calories per serving

Ingredients:

10oz (300g) minced beef
1 teaspoon oil
1 onion, chopped
2oz (60g) mushrooms, sliced
4oz (120g) swede, diced
4fl oz (120ml) stock
½oz (15g) cornflour
½ pint (300ml) skimmed milk
2oz (60g) blue cheese
6oz (180g) cooked rice

Method:

1) Shape the beef into patties. Lay on the rack of a grill pan and cook, turning once, until the fat stops dripping.

2) Heat the oil in a saucepan, add the onion and stir round. Cover and leave over a low heat for 5 minutes.

3) Stir the mushrooms, swede and stock into the saucepan. Crumble the beef into the vegetable mixture, stir round then cover the saucepan and leave over a low heat to simmer for 20-25 minutes.

4) When the beef has been cooking 15-20 minutes prepare the topping. Blend the cornflour together with the milk, bring to the boil, stirring all the time. Crumble the cheese into the sauce. Add the rice and stir over a low heat to warm through.

5) Spoon the beef and vegetables into a deep ovenproof dish, spoon the blue cheese rice evenly over and cook in a preheated oven, 375F, 190C, Gas Mark 5, for 15 minutes.

Selections per serving: ½ Bread, ¼ Fat, ¼ Milk, 2½ Protein, 1 Vegetable, 10 Optional Calories

TIP: *If preferred use curd cheese in place of fromage frais in the Kipper Pots.*

Kipper Pots

Serves 6
220 Calories per serving

Ingredients:

10oz (300g) kipper fillets
1 teaspoon margarine
4oz (120g) fromage frais
6oz (180g) cottage cheese
4 tablespoons skimmed milk
3 eggs
finely grated zest of ¼ lemon

Method:

1) Lay the kipper fillets in a pan, cover with cold water and place over a low heat, poach gently for 5 minutes. Using a fish slice remove the kipper fillets from the water and allow to cool. Remove the skin and any bones from the kipper fillets.

2) Lightly grease six ramekins, with the margarine.

3) Spoon the fromage frais, cottage cheese and milk into a liquidiser then process. Add the eggs to the liquidiser and process for a few seconds then pour the purée into a bowl.

4) Using a fork mix the lemon zest and fish into the purée. Mix well to break up the kipper fillets, but leave a few large flakes.

5) Spoon the kipper mixture into the ramekins and then transfer to a roasting tin. Pour sufficient hot water into the tin to reach about halfway up the sides of the ramekins. Bake at 350F, 180C, Gas Mark 4 for about 35 minutes or until set.

Selections per serving: 2½ Protein, 20 Optional Calories

Prawns with Spinach and Sweetcorn

Serves 2
265 Calories per serving

Ingredients:

12oz (360g) spinach
¾oz (20g) cornflour
8fl oz (240ml) skimmed milk
3oz (90g) sweetcorn
5oz (150g) peeled prawns
good pinch nutmeg
salt and pepper
1oz (30g) fresh breadcrumbs

Method:

1) Wash the spinach well then shake the leaves to remove excess water and place in a saucepan. Cover and cook over a moderate heat for 6-8 minutes until the leaves have collapsed and are cooked.

2) Drain the spinach very well. Press the spinach hard against the sides of a sieve then transfer to a chopping board and cut three or four times through the spinach – do not chop.

3) Place the cornflour in a saucepan and gradually blend in the milk. Bring to the boil stirring all the time. Cook for 2 minutes.

4) Add the sweetcorn and prawns to the sauce then season with the nutmeg, salt and pepper.

5) Spoon the spinach into a shallow flameproof dish, pour over the prawns and sweetcorn sauce then sprinkle the breadcrumbs over. Brown under a hot grill.

Selections per serving: 1¼ Bread, ¼ Milk, 2½ Protein, 2 Vegetable, 25 Optional Calories

---

TIP: *When skinning tomatoes, leave in the boiling water for no more than 40 seconds or they will become very soft.*

Plaice with Tomato and Leek

Serves 1
210 Calories per serving

Ingredients:

2 tomatoes
2 teaspoons margarine
1 small leek
3oz (90g) plaice fillet
salt and pepper
1 lemon wedge

Method:

1) Place the tomatoes in a small bowl, cover with boiling water and leave for 40 seconds. Remove the tomatoes from the hot water and slide off their skins. Cut in half and scoop out and discard the seeds, roughly chop the flesh.

2) Melt the margarine in a saucepan – just large enough to hold the plaice. Add the leek and stir-fry for 3-4 minutes until limp. Stir in the tomatoes and add 2 teaspoons water.

3) Lay the plaice on top of the vegetables, sprinkle with salt and pepper then cover and leave over a low heat for 7-8 minutes or until the fish is cooked.

4) Transfer the fish to a warm serving plate and increase the heat. Cook the vegetables, stirring all the time, until the liquid has evaporated. Spoon the vegetables round the fish and serve with a wedge of lemon.

Selections per serving: 2 Fat, 2 Protein, 2¼ Vegetable

Index